# Adventure Mountain Biking

# ADVENTURE MOUNTAIN BiKiNG

## TOURING • SPORT
## EXPEDITIONS

CARLTON REID

**The Crowood Press**

First published in 1990 by
The Crowood Press Ltd
Ramsbury, Marlborough
Wiltshire SN8 2HR

© Carlton Reid 1990

This impression 1991

**British Library Cataloguing in Publication Data**

Reid, Carlton
    Adventure mountain biking.
    1.   Mountainous regions. Cycling
    I.   Title
    796.6'0914'3

    ISBN 1 85223 388 5

Typeset by PCS Typesetting, Frome, Somerset
Printed in Great Britain at The Bath Press

# Contents

# Acknowledgements

Multiple thanks are due to the following people:

Jean and Albert Reid, Tom and Anne Craig, Dave Yates, Paul Chapman, Joe Waugh, Geoff Dobson and everyone at Steel's, Tym Manley, the SOS team, Janet Robertson, Matt Mills of Caratti Sport, Bob Boswell of Dawes, Nick Duncan of Madison, Dave Partridge of Serval Marketing, all at Rohan, Molly and Fran at Been Bag, everybody at Berghaus, all the people who answered my Viewpoint questions and last, but not least, Tim Hill must be heartily thanked for printing some of the photographs and for sitting for eleven hours at my VDU screen being constructively critical.

Gratitude is also expressed to the people who have ridden with Michael Craig and myself over the last few months. The following not only accompanied us on many a great day out they also kindly agreed to let themselves be photographed and included in this book:

Paul Arnold, Steve Bainbridge, Nick Cass, Stu Elsy, Mary Forrest, Ruth Forrest, Johnny Gates, Dave Goodwin, Alex Hayles, Mark Held, Tim Hill, Wendy Kessler, Brent MacDonald, Rob Orr, Rebecca Sanderson, Sarah Whitlock and Dave Yates.

All photographs are by Michael Craig, apart from those appearing on pages 48, 111, 112, 115, 151 and all line-drawings are by Janet Robertson.

I would like to thank Chris Townsend of *Wilderness Odyssey* and Tym Manley of *Mountain Biking UK* for publishing some of the material that appears in this book in the first place and for allowing me to use it again.

# Introduction

Unlike a couple of years ago there are now many books available on the sport and pastime of mountain biking. This one adds another volume to the list. As mountain biking is such a rapidly growing sport there is always going to be plenty of room for new treatments of the subject matter and hopefully this book will be seen as a worthwhile entry into the fray!

It will attempt to deal with certain topics in much more depth than the other books; although, of course, some other topics have had to be neglected and so this book could never claim to be the definitive manual of mountain biking. This difference in emphasis is because of my particular interests and is a natural outcome of being allowed a free-hand in coming up with the written material. I was not restricted to producing a mountain biking 'textbook' and whilst certain parts of the book could be viewed as instructional, the main *raison d'etre* of *Adventure Mountain Biking* is to offer advice and proffer inspiration. In this book there are no diagrams of bike frames telling the reader the names of the various parts of an ATB – these, the average mountain biker will already know. Whilst there is much the absolute beginner would find interesting within these pages I have written this book specifically for those riders who know what a bike is, know how to maintain it and, of course, know how to ride it.

Any semi-instructional work will lean towards the specialisation of the author. This work is no exception. Exotic, long distance, bike travel is my forte, so touring – in other words really getting off the road and exploring – is emphasised throughout. There are chap-

ters on inspiring you to get on out there, chapters on advanced navigation techniques for mastering unknown terrain, chapters on mountain clothing to protect you from the elements and so on and so forth. Interspersed with all this are various 'travelogues' and anecdotes that will hopefully entertain and enlighten at the same time. If because of reading this book just one person is inspired to go out and sample mountain bike touring for themselves then I shall consider the work a success!

Aspects of touring – short tours, equipment choice and expedition tours. Most people go on short tours – they do them at speed if they are in training for a race or slowly if they want to absorb the views, the atmosphere and the pleasure. The equipment chapter will deal with the sort of gear you may feel the urge to purchase for a longer trip – my suggestions are, however, entirely optional.

I define expeditions as any tour longer than a day. Admittedly this is a fairly loose definition – and maybe it even weakens the strength and emotiveness of the word – but at least this means I will not have to subdivide tours into weekend tours, week-long tours, three month tours, foreign tours, mountain tours, tow-path tours and so on. The use of the word expedition is therefore a catch-all phrase that will make even the simplest of weekend sorties sound like an adventure. Depending on your experience this is what it can be – a two day ride along the Peddars Way can be an adventure for somebody who has never done a cycle expedition before. Camping out by the side of the track can be exciting for even the most hardened of tourers but much more so for those new to the game. For old hands the dangers, worries and possible mishaps have to be greatly increased for the same feelings to arise.

I have decided not to devote a chapter to the history of mountain biking. Firstly, because this is a subject that needs more than a chapter if it is to be dealt with properly and secondly, because all the originators are still alive it is unnecessary for an outsider to rewrite the story. Readers who are interested in the early development of the sport both in America and in the UK are invited to turn to the Further Reading section where they will find listed the various books dealing with mountain bike history. This section is also quite broad – it deals with mountain biking as a sport and pastime in its own right, and so includes specific books on mountain biking, but it also lists books that cover associated subjects. For example, instead of a first-aid chapter in this book I have listed the various works available that deal with mountain injuries in general. Many works written with climbers, walkers and back-packers in mind are useful and so the Further

Reading section should not be seen as an after-thought, hidden away at the back of the book, but as an essential self-help course.

The views expressed in *Adventure Mountain Biking* will be my views, biased no doubt by the fact that no two people can have the exact self-same opinions. However, to temper this bias there will be a Viewpoints section after five of the chapters. Over a period of four months I interviewed some of the most influential personalities involved with mountain biking. Viewpoints is the edited-down result. Whilst I may have directed some of their answers by the particular questions I asked, their views may not be ones that I hold myself.

It should be noted that where bikes, products and items of equipment are mentioned in the text by trade name this does not imply an outright endorsement. The terms all-terrain bike, mountain bike, off-road bike and ATB will all be used interchangeably. There is no hidden meaning for this and I imply no subtlety of demarcation between the four – it simply means I have four ways of describing what is essentially the same type of machine.

# 1 One Big Adventure

It is a dark night. A shiny new mountain bike lies against the window of my local corner shop. A young lad – blond, freckled and dressed in a track suit – pulls the bike from where it was leaning. As he bunny-hops from the kerb his rear light smashes to the ground. After a quick glance back he speeds off. All of a sudden a little bulb flashes on in my head and I realise the lad has just stolen a bike right from under my nose – but by this time he is off round the corner and I would have no chance to catch him by giving chase. As I walk into the shop I can see the hapless owner – who is still oblivious to the loss of her machine – chatting with the shop assistant. I tell her that her bike has just been stolen. Her face drops and she glances over to the window where moments before she had left her machine. True enough it was not there. She sighs and then plods from the shop, shoulders hunched, head down.

Mountain bikes have revitalised the British bike-theft industry. A few years back the

Today everybody wants a mountain bike.

industry went through a bit of a depression because the market for second-hand sports bikes was not great. Today everybody wants a mountain bike, so suddenly the market is buoyant once more. Mountain bikes in London can be stolen, sold and stolen again within the space of an hour. Thieves work round the clock to ensure the voracious second-hand market is kept fed with machines.

The popularity of mountain biking is astounding. In just a few short years a heavy, fat-tyred, unsvelte off-road machine has achieved sales previously thought impossible this side of the bursting of the BMX bubble. The whole world and his dog appears to be riding a mountain bike. So why this sudden popularity? A hideously clever hype by the marketing people, perhaps? Or, are mountain bikes machines that answer real needs – that is to say wants metamorphosed into needs? It is a bit of both I should imagine. People needed the concept of what was later to be called the mountain bike, but it took the marketing people to identify this need. After all, the young West Coast Americans who stumbled upon the original concept had no idea their downhill cruisers would hijack the world of traditional cycling and would, in time, lead to a renaissance in bicycle ownership worldwide.

The raw concept had to be modified and streamlined and given an image of reckless abandon. The fact that hype – for once – almost lived up to expectations must be seen as quite some boon by the marketeers. Here was a product that almost sold itself (given the odd nudge now and then of course) and sold in

Mountain bikes have an image of reckless abandon.

numbers that soon gave rise to the first mountain biking millionaires. Real mountain bikes, such as the Fisher's, the Orange's, the Specialized's and the Marin's of this world, are selling in the tens of thousands. Yet this is actually only a small fraction of the total mountain bike market. In 1989 the British public bought nearly a million mountain bikes – granted, most were cheap machines that would crumble at the first taste of the great outdoors, but they were still mountain bikes.

So ATBs now account for as much as forty per cent of the total UK bike market – with real mountain bikes (models costing upwards of £300) accounting for about fifteen per cent. For a mix between marketing hype and genuine need this is an awful lot of units sold and no one could fault the *Cycle Trader Directory 1989*, the main bicycle trade paper, for claiming that '. . . the mountain bike has been responsible for the biggest upswing in cycling for years.'

This upswing has demonstrated that mountain bikes are famous. Famous and adored. For those of an earlier generation they conjure up images of the old, black trusty roadsters, fifty pounders that could be left out in the rain, jumped up and down on and still used for ever. For the younger generation they are BMX reborn. Brightly coloured stunt bikes that can jump, wheelie and hop like a bunny. For those people who fall between both extremes, the mountain bike is the well-geared cross-country cycle that can take us to places that two wheels have rarely been to before and which can make city riding a pleasure and not a pain.

I suppose in reality the mountain bike is a

Custom built bunny hopping.

Mountain biking is for all ages!

mixture of all these ideals. Strong (although, of course, not indestructible), resilient, safe, yet with an inbuilt capacity for fun. They are the leisure bikes of the eighties and nineties – bikes to tour upon, to cross-country race on, to street stomp with and above all else to enjoy cycling upon. For the novice and expert alike mountain biking is one big adventure.

In their own way ATBs have freshened up the bicycle industry – their bright colours and exciting, advertisable image epitomises all that is new and welcome on the cycle scene around the world. The new phenomenon of mountain biking – a surprise to many in the cycle trade – means more choice for consumers. Bikes and components have improved in quality. Machines have become more versatile.

At the cheaper end of the market the differences between a mountain bike and the type of sit-up-and-beg sports machine that were available before the ATB came along are not great. It is the concept that sells, not the actual end-product. But if the concept is bringing hordes of new people to cycling then it is a concept, a hype, a marketing game that is doing a great deal of good.

Women are especially attracted to mountain biking – perhaps because it is a new pastime – so men and women join on equal footing. Also, because cycling requires the rider to have an abundance of stamina it is a perfect sport for women, who generally have more of this attribute than men. Traditional cycling is cliquey and restricting and women may find the barriers put

Women are especially attracted to mountain biking.

up by 'those in the know' too daunting to break down. One female friend of mine, Sarah Whitlock, actually endured the tribulations of being the only woman cyclist in her local road racing club for quite a long time. She received very little encouragement from the men and because she happened to be slower than most of the male riders she would often be left at the back on club runs. The road cyclists only accepted her on their terms and even then only begrudgingly. Michael Craig, who took the photographs for this book, persuaded her to try mountain biking. She bought a Marin and has not been back on her road bike since. She finds the attitudes in mountain biking much more relaxed and the sport as a whole is far more open to women. In fact women are positively encouraged to join in. Day rides are not training runs – certain sections may be taken fast, just for the hell of it, but more normally the group goes at the pace of the slowest rider. This is not always the woman rider but, if it is, then at least she knows that the group will not tear off and leave her behind.

The mountain bike phenomenon – as well as creating a whole new market for the bicycle – is also affecting the bicycle industry in other ways. Racing and touring bikes are becoming more and more 'jazzy'; componentary is improving in leaps and bounds and the unit prices for all machines are now a few notches higher because of mountain biking. The cycle industry has much to thank those first Marin County enthusiasts for. More good quality bikes are being sold than ever before and the cheap ten-speed 'pseudo' ATB is taking over from the Sturmy Archer utilitarian bike as the ride-to-work machine. Prices are now quite high – a decade ago only the serious cycle enthusiasts would have ever dreamed of spending large amounts of money on bikes; now casual 'cyclists' with plenty of money to spare, think nothing of spending such sums. Mountain bikes do not compete with other bicycles but with other

items of leisure equipment – very often the people buying mountain bikes are also potential buyers for things such as skis, windsurfers and the like. These people are used to spending lots of money on consumer durables and leisure goods, and so £400 for a bright pink mountain bike is not seen to be extravagant.

The extra money being spent on the purchase of such machines is allowing many forward looking retailers to refit their shops in a manner more suited to their new image of being retailers of fashionable items of leisure equipment. This in turn attracts even more up-market buyers, eager to purchase from the new style shops. Retailers have realised that, unlike the BMX craze, the mountain bike phenomenon is not a passing fad. Mountain bikes are adult-orientated machines – not just geared-up BMXs – and they are not subject to the whims, fancies and short attention span of children. As the *Cycle Trader Directory 1989* says, 'For the first time in years the cycle trade has an up-market product, which has universal appeal, and is in universal demand. . . . The mountain bike is possibly the best thing to hit the trade for generations: far more so than the BMX boom.'

Mountain biking has produced its own heroes. First of all the Cranes hauled their bikes up Kilimanjaro and ever since then other cycling adventurers have completed equally intrepid trips. Britain even has the best racers in the world – Tim Gould and others are showing that we can beat the Americans at their own game. Skills are rapidly developing and many mountain bikers, completely new to any form of bicycle riding, are taking cycling in directions very different to those which most crystal-ball gazers would have predicted ten or fifteen years ago. Back then it was the up-market touring bike, and the attitudes that came along with it, that looked set to be the pattern for cycling in the eighties and nineties. This did not materialize. Today, instead of the high-tech

The mountain bike is the perfect touring machine.

British racers are now at the top of the hill when it comes to speed!

cycle tourist, it is the 'fluorescent' mountain biker who is the norm, and not the exception.

Paul Arnold, a Tyneside teacher in his early thirties, is perhaps typical of a new breed of people attracted to the sport that would not have been attracted to straightforward cycle touring or racing. He regularly spends a small fortune on his leisure activities and much of this budget now goes on mountain biking paraphernalia. He rides like he breathes – automatically and subconsciously, but he is always in total control of his machine – riding with him is an experience.

Normally I am relatively sane on a mountain bike – not quite staid but conservative at least – and the likelihood of me getting two feet of space between my tyres and the ground is quite rare. Paul Arnold changed all that. He will attempt things that would scare the skin tights off anybody else. He is so good that everybody who rides with him will try that little bit harder to succeed. After all, like in racing, if you do not go out with people better than yourself you will never improve.

His extra-strong machine – painted in mellow, pastel colours that do not really reflect his riding style – was relatively new when I went out cycling with him for the first time. It was to receive quite a christening in Chopwell Woods, a hilly expanse of local woodland. This may have been our first meeting but his reputation had preceded him. A mutual friend had warned us of Paul's lack of reasonable thought when it came to ATB stunting. His reputation really did live up to the reality – and whereas normally we would bomb around Chopwell fast

Mad mountain bikers are the norm, not the exception!

Paul the mad mountain biker!

and furious, with the odd bunny-hop thrown in for good measure, we would not normally seek out obstacles to deliberately 'head bang' over.

Paul soon altered that state of affairs. We came to an old disused quarry and Paul quickly located a terrifyingly steep descent. It was down a gravel slope where real control was out of the question. The only way you could miss the trees ten metres from the bottom was to flick the bike sideways – rather like a ski-plough turn – and hope you were going fast enough for the flick to register in the gravel. Paul sped down first, with me second, Alex third and Dave an apprehensive fourth. To one side of the trees lay a makeshift ramp, constructed of a large piece of plywood and bolstered up by stones. We all came down too fast to be able to see if there was anything on the downside of it so none of us attempted any stunts – not even Paul!

After reaching the bottom and quickly examining the feasibility of the jump Paul walked half-way back up the slope, positioned himself neatly on the back of his machine and came skidding down the gravel scree. The slope was at such an angle that a jump from the ramp would have to end in failure because of the space between the lip and the ground. Paul tried though and unceremoniously dumped himself and his machine two metres on the other side of the ramp. His flight had been brief but dramatic. He stood up and wiped the gravel dust from his clothes.

I too could see that the jump was impossible to execute without falling off, but instead of backing down – and egged on by the others – I made preparations for an attempt. I dragged my bike up the slope, wiped a gritty hand across my brow and with teeth well clenched I let go of the brakes and hurtled on down to the ramp. From here on in there was no turning back. To have not hit the jump would have led to more injury than doing it. An aborted attempt would mean hitting the ramp from the side with the brakes full on and this would not have done me any good. A straight line run-in was the only option. I just could not abort anyway – too many eyes were watching. Far better to injure myself, than be derided for not having had a go – a silly macho attitude of course, but one that is hard to avoid.

I hit the ramp at speed – one second I could see a gravel-peppered plywood sheet filling my wraparound shades and the next nothing but the slope two feet below. My front wheel dropped, I pitched violently forward and all of a sudden I was swimming in mid-air – arms flailing, legs gyrating and voice screaming at full blast. The bike smashed into the ground and I continued on through the air until I bounced on my shoulder into the gravel and rolled three or four times down to the bottom of the slope. It was not the most pretty of flights but at least all I had to show for it were some abrasions and half a pound of gravel in my shoes. My head had tucked in easily and the helmet that was firmly attached to it suffered not a scratch.

I lay still for a couple of seconds and then eased myself up, checking for cracks as I went – first on my body and then on my bike. Both were fine – even the forks had survived the impact. From behind came the sound of laughter – the laughter of an experience shared. Paul was in fits of giggles. I managed a relieved smile. So, this was what real head-banging was all about – I have never looked back. These kind of attitudes are common. Mountain biking can make anybody into a child again. This is not something to be sneered at – childlike qualities and childlike fun can be extremely beneficial to people who would normally consider themselves wholly mature. Mountain biking can be a release, a rejuvenating frolic, an expression of the inner child within us all.

Even the most staid and responsible of ATB expeditionists would not pass up the chance to take all the luggage off their bikes and play once in a while. Mountain bikes inspire play. They

Mountain bikes inspire play.

Step riding is fun – flat tyres are not!

suggest it and allow it to be put into practice. Fat tyres, sure brakes and a nimble, fast frame make even first-time riders feel secure enough to mess about. I remember the first thing I ever did on a mountain bike was to ride down a small flight of stairs. Whilst I would not normally have done such a thing on my touring bike my friend's mountain bike just shouted at me to do something silly on it. I cannot remember a sensible moment of riding since then!

Obviously more and more people will become converts to mountain biking – and with the fervour of converts they will preach to their friends and within no time everybody will own and use a mountain bike for pleasure.

There is a famous press photograph, from quite a while back, of Edward Heath, the then Prime Minister, falling backwards off a skateboard – the craze of the day, a craze that almost, but not quite, became mainstream. There is no known pictorial record of the present incumbent of Number 10 Downing Street doing the same on a mountain bike. Nevertheless the ATB is now firmly within the mainstream and it will not go away. Skateboarding died a death years ago; mountain biking is alive and kicking and looks set to be around for as long as people have legs!

Before you get on with the rest of the book it may be worthwhile reading about the personalities who will be putting forth their opinions in the Viewpoint sections that will be accompanying five of the chapters. The people I interviewed for these sections are the most influential set of people in mountain biking today. Their opinions are important – they will shape how mountain biking evolves.

**Geoff Apps** could be said to be the original British mountain biker. He was riding a 'cross-country bicycle' when I was still in nappies. He is the director of Cleland Cycles and the president of the Cross-Country Cycle Club.

**David Baker** rides for the professional Peugeot team. He is by training a cyclo-cross rider but along with Tim Gould he has rapidly gained experience, and many wins, in the field of mountain bike racing.

**Tom Bogdanowicz** works in London for ABC news but he also writes for most of the cycling magazines. He has been fixated by bikes ever since his father put him in a tandem side-car.

**Tim Davies** rides for Schmoo's Cycles. He was the 1989 Welsh Cyclo-cross Champion. In 1986 he rode a track-bike at the Edinburgh Commonwealth games. Tim now rides a Clockwork Orange very quickly.

**Max Glaskin** started cycling as a cub newspaper reporter chasing fire-engines. He was editor of *Bicycle Magazine* and the *Bicycle Buyers Guide* from 1984 to 1986. Together he and Jeremy Torr reorganised NORBA into the

MBC. Max also co-wrote *Mountain Biking* (Pelham Books, 1988) with Jeremy and is a regular contributor to *Winning* magazine.

**Errol Drew** was one of the driving forces behind the creation of Madison Cycles, the first European company to produce a mass-market mountain bike.

**Tim Gould** is primarily a cyclo-cross rider but he has also been racing mountain bikes since May 1988. He is a top professional rider and has won the punishing Three Peaks Cyclo-cross race five times. He rides for the Peugeot team.

**Nigel Jackson** discovered mountain biking in the early 1980s with his wife, Wendy and they were inspired to take up expeditioning. So far they have travelled in India, Nepal, Pakistan, France, Switzerland and Sardinia. Aside from travelling they are also part of the bike test team for *Mountain Biking UK*.

**Mike Kloser**, rides for MS Racing and is the ex-World Champion (Crans Montana). He has also won the 200-mile Iditabike cross-Alaska race. In 1989 he won the Carlsberg British Mountain Bike Championships held in Aviemore. He has been riding a mountain bike competitively since 1985 and comes from Vail, Colorado, USA.

**Drew Lawson** is the marketing guru behind Muddy Fox. Along with Ari Hadjipetrou he has created one of the most well-known brands of mountain bike in the world.

**Matt Mills** was joint winner of the "Fat-tyre Five" mountain bike series in 1985. He now works as marketing co-ordinator for Caratti Sport of Bristol, importers of Specialized bikes and accessories. After a bad accident in 1986 he quit racing but decided to take it up again in 1988. He races for the Specialized squad.

**Deb Murrell** rides for the Two Wheels Good/Dave Yates team based in Leeds and is definitely one of the best woman riders around. She won the first race she ever entered – the Quantock Quiver in 1987 – and has not looked back since.

**Lester Noble** has been an active mountain biker since 1985. He was the first British rider to finish in the gruelling 1987 World Championships. Along with a partner, he used to design and import the Tushingham range of bikes. He is now designing and importing Oranges (bikes not fruits!)

**Arthur Phillips** runs the Glentress Mountain Bike Centre which hires mountain bikes out to visitors to Peebles. He has been involved in the hiring of mountain bikes since 1986 and now has two separate mountain bike centres in the Borders region.

**Paul Skilbeck** is an active outdoor sports enthusiast and a one-time Australian road racer. Paul won his first mountain bike event after borrowing a bike from Paul Hinton. He beat the best of London's cycle couriers. He now rides for the Fisher-Chainsport team.

**John Stevenson** is deputy editor of *Mountain Biking UK* and technical guru to boot. He used to be the manager of the TWG shop in Leeds and is the founder of the Yorkshire Mountain Bike Club.

**Dave Yates** – *see* Chapter 9.

# VIEWPOINTS

*How big a part do you think ATBs have played in revitalising the British bicycle industry?*

**Geoff Apps** 'The current British bicycle trade owes a great deal to the ATB. This fact indicates to me that there was a vast potential market which was dissatisfied with the bikes available ten years ago, when nearly all bikes were drop handlebar, racing style bikes. The trade still does not recognise where its main market potential lies, and it is about to shoot itself in the foot again by predominantly producing race orientated ATB designs.'

**Tom Bogdanowicz** 'ATBs have been almost

entirely responsible for revitalising the bicycle industry after the demise of BMX. The only other serious input has been from triathlon bikes. The bike shops that brought in mountain bikes in the 80s are the ones that have expanded.'

**Errol Drew** 'Bicycles were increasing in fashion even before the advent of ATBs, but it is certainly thanks to the latter that there has been a major boost in interest from the public.'

*How many mountain bikes were you building four years ago? And how many now?*

**Dave Yates** 'It has gone up by a factor of perhaps five. We started building ATBs in 1983 and we have been building them steadily ever since – and we have certainly noticed that we are selling more and more.'

*Do you think mountain biking is perceived as being too macho for women, i.e. is it sexist? If so what can be done about this?*

**John Stevenson** 'Cycle sport in general is unwelcoming to women, because its current attitudes were set in store in the 1950s. Mountain biking is an ideal activity for women since it requires skill and endurance and can be enjoyed at any level from pottering round the Dales, to racing, to taking off across Africa. The MTB racing world is, I think, very open to women riders. The problem is that a lot of dealers treat women like idiots – only when this changes will things improve.'

**Deb Murrell** 'In relation to other sports it must be one of the least sexist, but it is by no means totally free from sexism. It is certainly less sexist than other branches of cycling and as a racer I experience little sexism, although I have been successful and I feel this has helped overcome certain prejudices. It is one of the few

sports where women compete at the same time as men thus maintaining an equal chance to compete. Most male mountain bikers are keen to see women's racing take off and encourage efforts like the women's mountain bike network Vixens. This network, although only in its early days, is proving successful at encouraging and linking women new to mountain biking. It now has over one hundred members.

Away from the racing scene women mountain bikers are open to much of society's in-built sexism. After leaving school most women give up sport and exercise. Those who continue and particularly those who enjoy a physically demanding sport such as mountain biking risk labels such as odd, weird or masculine. Unless they have a supportive circle of like-minded friends, a woman can very quickly feel isolated. This is a major barrier to encouraging women to take up mountain biking for leisure, let alone racing. Until society's attitudes change little can be done to stop the verbal, sometimes physical, abuse that women cyclists have to put up with from some men.

The best advice I can offer is to practise some suitably cutting phrases and to don the most intimidating pair of shades they can find. The latter usually deters abusive men and if it does not you are suitably equipped to deal with most exchanges.'

**Wendy Jackson** 'I feel that the "macho" image is less well-pronounced these days – people are seeing the sport for what it is – fun. Many women are possibly *more* likely to take up mountain biking than serious road riding. I have been approached several times for advice by women interested in buying mountain bikes, who realise that here is a bike that they can enjoy themselves on, without having to go very fast or very far, or look like a serious biker in order to be taken seriously as a cyclist. I also think that as mountain biking is still in its infancy, women feel that they can enter into the sport on equal terms with men who are just starting out too.'

*Mountain biking has taken off in a big way. Was this sudden surge a surprise to you at all?*

**Drew Lawson** 'No, this is what we have aimed and planned for all these years. If it had been a surprise we would have been idiots. It is what we wanted and what we set out to achieve. We could not predict exactly when it would happen but we knew there was a justifiable market there. We got the concept of mountain biking popularised – and we knew it would happen. As no one else was prepared to do anything it was up to us to popularise it. And as it became more and more popular people jumped on the bandwagon and they started to put money in and even the big boys eventually put their money in.

Mountain biking is above all else a fun activity. Yet often the image that mountain bike companies put out in their adverts is all wrong – to show people going *uphill* is a total waste of time, it is not why people buy bikes. If you go out and do an ad about a car or a jeep you don't see people taking the engine apart or changing the tyres – you see them having fun. Uphill is not fun for most people, it may be for purist cyclists but that is not the market they are after. The trouble is most of these companies are run by purist cyclists and they see the advantages of mountain bikes as being able to go uphill. I do not. I see the advantages of getting there so you can come *downhill* and in all our ads you will never see anybody going uphill. You do not see car adverts with people filling up with petrol – it is just not the nice side of driving.'

# 2 Navigation Techniques for Mountain Bikers

(Where Am I?)

On bright, sunny days the ability to navigate yourself successfully across the hills is important. On winter days, when the evenings draw in quickly and the weather can descend suddenly, such skills are imperative. There are enough courses, videos and books available for you to be able to learn how to traverse a minefield in a snowstorm. However, if you do not fancy these then read on; you may learn something that could save your life one day. This is not melodrama – just ask any Mountain Rescue Team.

Navigation is not difficult. It is not a hidden art but it is a useful method of deduction that can help you if you are lost. 'Lost', however, is an emotive word and many fine navigators will tell you that there is no such condition – indeed, 'temporarily unsure of your whereabouts' is often the best euphemism to use!

Learning how to use a compass is simple. It can easily be mastered indoors and a modicum of common sense is all that is needed. However, the ability to use and interpret a map is a skill that can only truly be mastered when you are actually outside examining the real landscape and comparing it to the diagrammatic representation. Visualising ground features from two-dimensional lines on a map is difficult for most people at first, but through much trial and error a good level of map-to-ground proficiency can easily be reached.

Most people want to get to the compass first, as if it is a magical beacon that will always point the best way home; but first it is useful if we examine a few basic land forms pertaining to mountain bikers and how they are portrayed on the map. It must be stressed that this chapter can only act as an introduction to navigation and if you wish to cycle on very rough or remote terrain it would be advisable for you to become thoroughly knowledgeable in navigation – and map work in particular. There is no better method of learning than to take a local Ordnance Survey (OS) map out on to some simple terrain that you know well, and to self-test yourself by matching map features with those on the ground. The 1:50,000 (Landranger) is the most useful scale but if a trip can be covered by one or two 1:25,000 maps then so much the better.

The basic land forms that pertain especially to mountain bikers are hills. There are plenty of times when it is appropriate to use map and compass skills when away from hilly country but it is when you are out on the slopes that these skills really come into their own. On featureless terrain a compass bearing can be followed if absolutely necessary but more normally there is often a linear feature – such as a river – that you can follow to maintain your desired direction. On the hills good map reading ability is the skill that really makes the most difference.

The most common mistake in basic non-compass navigation is misreading the inclination of hills – are those contour lines suggesting an uphill struggle, or a downhill wheeze? For walkers this information is important; it enables them to evaluate how much time they will spend

Where to now?

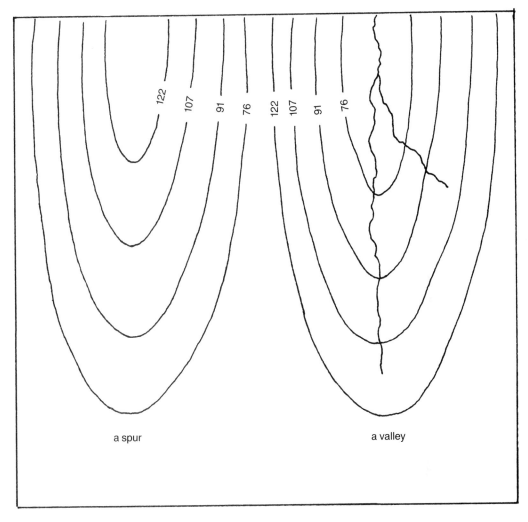

a spur                  a valley

Difference between a spur and a valley or re-entrant.

walking. The same is true for bikers – except that prior evaluation of a timing for a downhill section is likely to be much less accurate. The speed at which the rider is able to skim rocks and the lack of terrain information on the map can mean that the timing is either much faster than expected, or conversely agonisingly slow. Walkers, thanks to formulas such as Naismith's, have a much greater accuracy capability. This particular formula helps walkers to fix an 'esti-mated time of arrival' – as yet no mountain biking version has been developed, but given the variables mentioned above this is not very surprising!

Inability to tell uphill from downhill on a map does not give the prospective map reader much confidence! It is important to know whether the map is representing a spur (a high land feature projecting from a mountain range) or a re-entrant (a shallow valley running into a hill, kill and which should be avoided. The lip of the cliff is the jagged edge, not the open-ended section.

**Warning:** it should be noted that some foot-paths descend cliffs by tortuous routes unsuitable or dangerous for bikes – on some maps these paths are marked inaccurately and are shown going over cliffs. You should not be on footpaths anyway but if you ever have to cut a trip short and find from the map that a footpath would be the simplest way down, remember that terrain which may be relatively safe for a slow-moving walker can kill an over-zealous mountain biker.

Things happen very quickly in mountain biking. Route choice is often made at the very last second, so the pre-selection of routes is virtually impossible unless you already know the paths which are distinct and offer the best of all possible rides. Knowing your exact location is therefore always problematic. The simplest way to ensure you do not stray too far off course is to have your map folded small, to keep it handy and to constantly reset it so the land features underwheel are represented in the same manner on the map. Try to memorise each turn-off you make from your route – or if possible, actually reset your map soon after you turn off. Usually the deviation is too exciting for bikers to bother with this – which is fair enough – but it is expedient for me to advise people at least to try!

Shooting off down a steep hill tests both the rider and the bike.

often between two spurs). There are a number of ways of getting it right. For instance, at a glance you can see where the moving water features are running. Rivers and so forth do not normally course their way up spurs or along the tops of hills. Therefore, if you see a river on the map, the chances are that the feature it is running along is some sort of valley. Another way of differentiating between hills and valleys is to check the direction of the contour numbers on the map. They are written so they are read facing uphill. Alternatively you can compare the values of the contour numbers which are given at regular intervals along each contour line. The rate at which the numbers are either gaining or losing in numerical value indicates both the direction and steepness of the slope.

One map feature that should be especially noted is indicated by little black jagged lines jutting out of a slope. These are cliffs which can

# SETTING THE MAP

**Note:** to understand the following it would be useful if you had a protractor-type compass and OS map in front of you.

Setting the map is important for your visualisation and orientation. It can be done using the

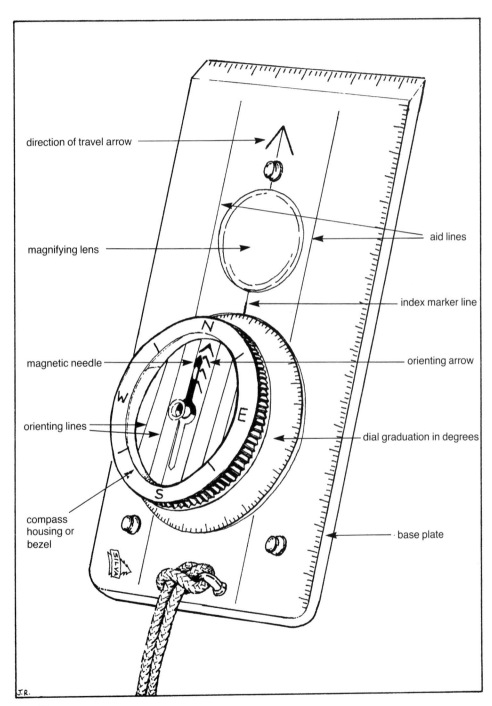

direction of travel arrow

aid lines

magnifying lens

index marker line

magnetic needle

orienting arrow

orienting lines

dial graduation in degrees

compass
housing or
bezel

base plate

The Silva compass.

compass (simply orientate the map to the north) if you are in poor visibility conditions; but it is much more likely that you will set the map by sight. To do this, turn the map until the features you can see all around you are in the same position as they are on the map. This may mean that all the lettering is upside-down; this does not matter. It is far more important to have an accurate pictorial representation of the ground in front of you rather than a map that has the wording correctly orientated, but from which you have to mentally turn the features the other way up. Some walkers prefer to be able to read off all the names of the cols, crags, crevices and so on that they pass, but on a mountain bike the same features whizz past at quite a speed and so trying to ascertain their names ceases to be quite as important.

# THE COMPASS

Now we can move on to using the compass. As stressed above, it is important to realise that this instrument is not the be-all and end-all of navigation – it will not always save you. Compasses can be inaccurate to quite a frightening degree. To minimise such inaccuracy buy a reputable brand (for instance Silva) and check it against a compass you know to be 100 per cent accurate. To do this note whether the north needles are pointing in the same direction on both compasses – do not, of course, have the compasses within magnetic range of each other – mark the direction of each north on a piece of paper instead.

Ensure that the area you are cycling through does not adversely affect the magnetic needle

'Well, if this isn't Ben Nevis then I'm lost!'

Visibility will not always be perfect.

of the compass. The Cuillin Ridge of Skye is a famous example of an area that can send compass needles haywire, but there are other areas that have similar local metal deposits and hence navigational irregularities. Also, you must of course always store and use your compass away from metallic or magnetic objects. For example, do not be too surprised if you veer wildly off course if you sight your compass whilst straddling a bicycle or leaning against an iron gate. It must also always be borne in mind that if you are not totally accurate in your compass work an error of just a couple of degrees over a distance can lead to a wholly misleading destination. Even if you are quite accurate a spoilage of four degrees either side is the norm – this means that for every kilometre covered the person following the compass will be seventy metres off course! Therefore do not rely on the compass to do all your navigating for you – use it only when really necessary and always make sure you are spot on with your bezel turns.

A compass does come in handy, however, when selecting the right choice of varying routes. For example, it is useful if you come to a junction and you are not too sure which path you should take but you can tell from the map that it is the north-westerly path you have to follow; or when the visibility is so bad you have to get off the bike and walk for safety reasons; or when you want to cycle in a dead straight line instead of going in circles. In this last circumstance – for instance if you forgot your map but you know there are no crags to fall off – then it is the compass and not your sense of direction that should be trusted. Otherwise a compass is almost superfluous; however, for those rare occasions when it will be needed, the basics of finding bearings and such like are given below.

# Basic Compass Work

If you do not know where you are and you cannot spot any identifiable features or landmarks that can be found on your map (for instance on a very dark night or if you are on a featureless plain) then you could be in trouble. If the light fails and you are in crag country where there are no paths, get off the bike and inch your way back to safety. If the way is relatively safe then follow a single bearing until you reach an identifiable feature – perhaps a road or track – in the British Isles you are never more than five miles or so from a metalled road or a good track.

However if you have a map, a compass and can spot two or more landmarks that can also be identified on the map then you will easily be able to find your approximate position by re-section. From there you can select a route by taking a bearing from the map and following it on the ground. Of course, if you can spot two features and match them to the map then you are not lost anyway! However, if you still feel you need the reassurance of a compass, this is how you use it.

Select two landmarks that are well apart, preferably at right angles to each other. Take your compass in the palm of your non-dominant hand and point the travel arrow at one of your features or landmarks. Sight along the travel arrow by squinting and then slowly bring the compass down to chest level, keeping it steady all the time. Now twist the compass housing until the north needle and the northwards-pointing orientating arrow (in the middle of the compass housing) match. The bearing of this first landmark is the number that is situated above the index marker line (the little notch in the housing that would form the lengthwise continuation of the travel arrow). Memorise this number and then take the bearing for the other landmarks.

These bearings are magnetic, or compass, bearings. Because of the constantly changing

Taking a bearing using a normal Silva compass.

nature of the Earth's magnetic field, magnetic bearings vary by a few degrees from true map, or grid, bearings. To convert magnetic bearings to grid bearings you have to remove this magnetic variation – it will be about 6.5 degrees. Therefore, if you used a trig point on the top of an identifiable hill and the mouth of a lake for your sighting points and your respective bearings were 86 and 327 degrees then the corresponding grid bearings are 79.5 and 320.5 degrees. Bear in mind though that one half of a degree is neither here nor there on the type of compass used here. There is a mnemonic to help you remember to remove the variation: MUGS – **M**agnetic **U**nto **G**rid **S**ubtract.

To find your position in relation to these two (or three) identifiable features, take the first grid bearing you memorised and set it on to the compass dial. Put the compass on to the map. Place the direction line (the side edge of the

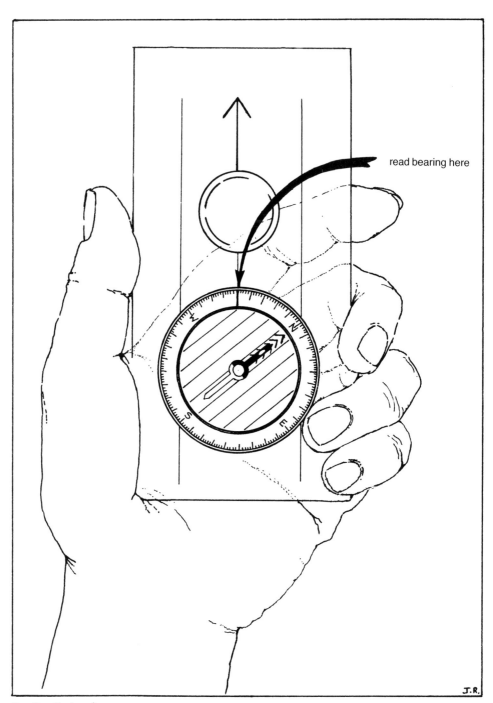

read bearing here

Reading the bearing.

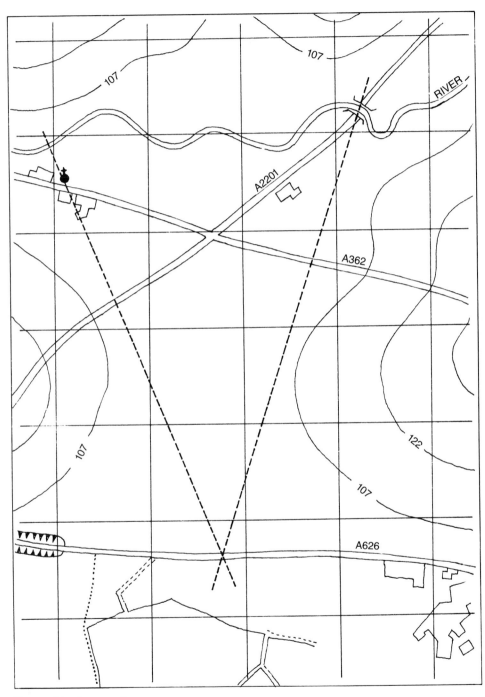

Your position by resection.

Mist can disorientate the unwary mountain biker.

compass base plate which is parallel to the travel arrow) over the first landmark and balance it on this point. Now swivel the compass until the orientating lines, inside the compass housing and pointing north, become parallel with the grid lines of the map. Where the edge of the compass lies now makes a line from the landmark to your approximate position. Repeating this process for the second and third landmarks will clarify this position still further.

Now you know where you are you can select a route. If finding your destination is a problem – for instance if the mist comes down or if you miscalculated how long you would be out and it is now dark, then one option open to you is to follow a compass bearing taken from the map. First you need to know your position. Try the above method (if at all possible) or search around to attempt to find a readily identifiable object, feature or landmark. A box search would help with the latter – get off the bike (leave a companion there so you do not lose your machine) and walk compass north for ten paces, turn east for ten more, then south for twenty, west for twenty, north for thirty, east for thirty, south for forty and so on until something is found. Alternatively just walk compass straight. If the terrain is difficult and visibility is nil and if you are injured or shivering then it is best not to travel at all but to stay put and climb into your bivvysac. However, if you do not panic and are sensible in where you put your feet, it should not be too difficult to get down to a road. Only bivvi for the night if it is the very last option. After all, if you climb into your bag because the mist has descended then you may be lying there for a week or two – mountain fog can last for days!

Let us assume you now know your position and you want a route which has to be navigated by a compass. Look at the map and take bearings from it in short steps until you reach your eventual destination – do not take a bearing from your position to a home point two miles away; the 'drift' of inaccuracy will pull you way off course. Move from obvious small landmark to obvious small landmark. This means taking a bearing to an obvious feature (for example the junction of two streams) – when you get there you know exactly where you are and so you can start the process again. Alternatively you can make a deliberate error in following your bearing – aim off to one side of where you want to go and then when you reach a linear feature turn in the opposite direction to this original 'error'. Try always to use linear features, such as rivers, field boundaries and so on as a definite means of guidance. To move from landmark to landmark, select your next destination and pinpoint your present one. With the compass edge link the two up, using the travel arrow as the direction of travel at all times. Keep the compass flat and steady; then swivel the housing until the interior orientating lines become parallel to the map grid lines. Read off the bearing. Now you must convert this grid (map) bearing into a magnetic (compass) one. This time add the 6.5 degrees. (The mnemonic for this is GUMA: Grid Unto Magnetic Add.) Swivel yourself around until the north point of the needle aligns itself with the north point of the interior orientating arrow. To set off in the right direction, ensure the needles stay aligned and move in the direction that the travel arrow suggests.

These are the two most basic compass route-finding methods. There are more advanced methods and many variations of skirting obstacles with the aid of a compass but these two will get you going.

In the past there have been mountain bike 'orienteering' races and on these map and compass skills really can be honed to perfection. Yet it is still the map that is the most important tool. Concentrate on perfecting your landscape spotting before you graduate on to more advanced compass techniques. Throughout the whole of your active life you may never

No through road. Should we be here?

have to use a compass in anger. Those people who neglect map work in favour of compass training are those most likely to find themselves 'temporarily unsure of their whereabouts'.

# 3 Access and Conservation

(Should I be Here in the First Place?)

It cannot be overstated that access – our passport to the great outdoors – is the most important consideration for those mountain bikers who venture away from the tarmac. The future of the sport, in its real off-road form, depends upon free access.

Many people who buy mountain bikes do so for the pose value; most do not actually venture off-road. However, the proportion of those who do so is growing all the time and although when British mountain biking started, the illegality of races and so forth was not really noticed, the same cannot be said today. With the increase in numbers has come notoriety. No longer is mountain biking considered a fringe or eccentric activity – it is now a part of the mainstream and so no deviance from the Mountain Bike Club code of practice (*see* the Off-road Code at the end of this chapter) is allowed.

Bike access to footpaths, hill country and other areas has always been fairly complicated, however, before mountain biking came along the rules were not generally enforced – there just were not enough off-roaders for there to be any real problems. Today these rules are enforced on a regular basis and in some cases, which are not as isolated as could be hoped, bikes have been banned altogether. The complicated access rules have to be studied in depth to see exactly what rights we do and do not have. There are definite places, paths and tracks where mountain bikers, or any other cyclists, can and cannot go. Many good-looking routes are closed to us. Some mountain bikers do not

like this state of affairs and the breaching of highway by-laws is an all too common occurrence. However, if mountain biking is to continue as a legitimate and vibrant off-road activity, we must realise that upsetting walkers and antagonising local councils and farmers is not a good way to plan for the future.

We must all be ambassadors for the sport and must aim, wherever possible, to stay within the strict letter of the law. This can often be a difficult task and whilst I am obliged to advise you of the details of the highway by-laws I do not expect mountain bikers to take full heed of them. Realistically speaking the by-laws are tough to enforce and cyclists will basically go where they want – this attitude may lead to blanket bans for mountain bikes in certain areas but such restrictions, no matter how strongly they were worded, would not deter everybody. Footpaths, despite in effect being closed to two-wheeled modes of transport, are cycled upon regularly and therefore, whilst I will list some of the definitions of routes we can and cannot cycle upon, I accept that mountain bikers will usually ignore them if the route is a good one. I neither condone nor condemn this; I simply recognise the fact. It is however, in their own interest that mountain bikers act more responsibly than this. Britain is crisscrossed by a veritable maze of fantastic off-road routes that are completely legal to ride upon. There is often no need to cycle in forbidden territory – such routes as the West Highland Way in Scotland, Mastiles Way in Yorkshire, the Ridge-

There are many fantastic off-road routes in Britain.

way in southern England and Salter's Road in Northumberland can be extremely testing and satisfying rides and are by no means isolated examples. We must remember that mountain biking is a newcomer to the outdoor scene and that we are still a minority sport compared to such pursuits as recreational walking. Whilst I do not advocate the 'shrinking violet syndrome' – for example acceding to each and every missive from the Rambler's Association, no matter how absurd – I do believe that we should be more understanding of the rights of other outdoor users – as long as they recognise our rights too, of course.

If rules are to be imposed on us it will be by the authorities, egged on by the walking, farming and horse-riding lobbies. We can try to negotiate settlements favourable to mountain

biking, but, in the long run, if we antagonise the walkers, the local councils and the farmers, then very restrictive rules may be imposed on us from above. Despite the fact that different outdoor users are often in conflict with each other it should be pointed out that we ought to be forging closer links with such groups. This is because water privatisation, in some areas, is going to lead to severe restrictions for *all* groups and instead of the present fighting there should be a common bond. This, however, is more of a pipe dream than a constructive proposal for guaranteeing the rights of all outdoor users!

Trespassing on ground that we are not entitled to be on is one thing, but rampant and wilful destruction of the areas we cycle through can in no way be excused. Skidding, broad-

Farmland can be cycled through if there are rights of way.

41

slides, wheel-locks and other such mud-churners should not be executed whilst out in the wilds at all.

There are two ways that bikes can damage the surface of the ground. The first is by the force of compression – the weight of the rider and bike acting vertically by gravity. This compressive force pushes down on the ground and can squeeze the tiny air pockets out of the soil. This in turn can mean that the soil will tend to soak up less rain-water and if this soil is situated on a slope then the risk of gullying due to run-off and erosion is increased. The soil organisms, in rare cases, may also be affected; plant growth may become less vigorous too. However, in time, and through the action of worms and so forth, the soil can regain its air pockets – if the damage does not occur frequently that is. Soil has a certain degree of elasticity, but it fractures if several riders run over the same ground in rapid succession. The cure for this is to restrict the numbers going out on to the hills at any one time.

The second damaging force, and by far the most destructive, is the ripping and tearing action of a shear force. This is caused by skidding, wheel-locks, cornering and acceleration and results in vegetation and soil being pushed sideways. Shear forces can visibly scar the ground and will reduce the vigour of surface vegetation growth; root systems may also be disturbed. This in turn damages the soil even more as new growth is restricted and the soil may be less able to withstand further pressure.

Both damage-creating forces can be lessened by increasing the tyre footprints of your

Grass will not be damaged by mountain bike passage.

Hard-packed dirt is good mountain biking terrain.

machine – by reducing the pressure in the inner tubes. Compressive forces cannot be avoided by individual riders. Many of the shear ones can. Basically, be thoughtful. As soil and grass is more prone to damage when it is wet, you should also try to avoid environmentally-sensitive areas if they are water-logged or extremely greasy.

Technical trespass may be tolerated if we are kind both to the environment and to our fellow countryside users; damage will not be so easily tolerated. Therefore we must aim to preserve the landscape we travel through. Four-wheel drive vehicles and trails motorbikes have been completely banned in many places, mostly because of the obvious and very real damage they cause. This could quite easily happen to us and bans due to the risk of damage may be enforced very strongly indeed. For instance, in some areas where trials motorbikes are banned the police have similar machines and so it is no longer the case that by-law offenders can speed away. Mind you the police will be damaging the ground just as much as the offending riders! If mountain bikers are not to be viewed in the same light as motorised off-road vehicles, which have laid waste great swathes of the countryside, we must adopt a low-impact approach to the environment we travel through. Granted 2.125's are less damaging to the environment than Land Rover tyres, horse's hooves and hordes upon hordes of walking boots – however, mountain bikers tend to be visually stunning, have adopted to ride around on strangely-equipped machines and generally appear to be having a lot of fun and so have created a high profile for themselves. Our fat tyres and aggressive looking handlebars also suggest the appearance of a trials motorbike.

Even if every single mountain biker kept within the local by-laws, rode reasonably and generally acted with the considerations of others in mind, then we would still raise the hackles on some people. They often do not like the way we look or the way we have decided to visit the great British landscape. And as soon as one single, irresponsible and rowdy off-road rider comes along all their doubts, apprehensions and blinkered fears are confirmed. In many ways it is a no-win situation and because we are a new outdoor sport it will take time, and much effort, to persuade others to view us as a legitimate and responsible group of outdoor users. You can do your bit by riding only on legal rights of way, by acting considerately at all times and by adopting the low-impact approach. Group sizes should also be kept to the minimum. Four or five riders should be the most that ever venture out in one pack – even just five riders can look very intimidating and so groups larger than this should think of segmenting their numbers a bit more. Nevertheless, mountain bikers have effectively been banned from entering certain areas around the country – for instance, the Burnham Beeches and the Quantock Hills are currently no-go areas. Popular routes are regularly closing to fat tyres. Often such blanket bans are a result of just a few irresponsible mountain bikers who pay little regard to the needs or concerns of others. Their bad or negligent behaviour ruins it for us all.

Despite what I have said above, damage to the environment is actually quite low on the list of grievances drawn up by walkers and the like – this is possibly because they know that they themselves do far more damage to the environment, for instance look at the great scars walkers have created in the North York Moors and other places, just by the passage of their boots. Much higher on the list is the aggressive behaviour of many mountain bikers. Instead of a vocalised greeting and a cheery wave the walker often just sees a fluorescent flash as the biker speeds past oblivious to the impression he or she is creating. When this single flash is followed by a whole host of other day-glo flashes – all tearing past at breakneck speed –

then the impression generated is one of disgust. This need not be the case – a touch more politeness and care would make the world of difference. Remember, many people go into the hills for peace and quiet and solitude. By all means go fast if you want to but at least slow down when you spot walkers or horse riders.

This chapter will attempt to explain where mountain bikers can and cannot legally go. It is a complex subject, and one with many abbreviations. You could read and digest everything and still be none the wiser when you are actually out there looking at the ground. Unless you study the local definitive 1:25,000 or 1:10,000 maps (available for viewing at your local County Council offices) you may be unwittingly and regularly, committing offences. What may seem like a very wide, easy-to-ride public track to you may in fact be marked as a private road by the definitive map and would therefore be legally out of bounds to fat-tyre travellers. Even if you do become *au fait* with all the terms – BOATs, RUPPs, UCRs and so on – you may still be on the wrong side of the law if you do not check out the definitive maps. Ordnance Survey maps sometimes relay the wrong classification or may be out of date and therefore a trip down to your local County Council planning office (or library) may be necessary to search out the definitive map and to determine the exact routes of tracks and bridleways. The local council will possibly employ a rights of way officer and so accurate access information may be easy to obtain.

As the rights of way officer would tell you, every inch of Britain is owned by somebody. Technically speaking, in England, if we stray from the path or the bridleway we are trespassing and the landowner could sue us for any damage done or deemed to be have been done. Routes that follow rights of way allow us to travel along them to reach a particular destination but we must not stop, or even turn back but progress from A to B as quickly and as quietly as possible. Even stopping to mend a puncture is, in theory, disallowed – a stranded mountain biker could be asked to keep on moving if the landowner wished to adhere to the strict lettering of the law. Most would not, but do not cause a fuss if an inconsiderate one does.

Trespass is not actually a criminal offence but instead is a civil wrong, or 'tort' and the landowner has the right to sue if the trespasser does any damage, or, as was stated above, is deemed to have done so. Nominal damages will be awarded to a landowner by the courts for the inconvenience of a trespass. The landowner can also take out injunctions against trespassers who are a 'continuous nuisance' and he or she has the right to evict anybody straying on to his or her land. This legal eviction can be executed with as much force as is deemed reasonable and necessary. Landowners should at first ask the trespasser to leave but if he or she refuses to then the eviction can take place. Trespass on Ministry of Defence lands, on the other hand, is often a criminal offence – especially when firing is taking place – as well as being unnecessarily dangerous! Accidental trespass on MoD land would be difficult as most ranges or bases are well protected and cordoned off. When wire fencing is neither appropriate nor necessary the area, if a firing range, will be marked off by flags. Red flags denote a 'live' situation. Riders on Salisbury Plain, Dartmoor, the Otterburn area of Northumberland or the East Norfolk coast near Blakeney should take especial precautions when taking part on rides that may stray, accidentally, on to MoD land. I have lived near both of the last two areas and normally it is quite clear cut where the MoD land starts (especially if you study the maps well – danger areas are clearly marked as such). The day may come, however, when a mountain biker finds him- or herself right in the middle of a firing range. Whilst there it is likely that he or she will face two major risks – one of being shot at or bombed upon and the other of being seriously

Mountain bikes are tough and aggressive machines.

fined and possibly imprisoned. Check up on Chapter 2 if you feel the urge to skirt MoD land at any stage in your riding career!

Restricted access is also the case for hilltops and pathless uncultivated terrain – this includes 'open country', which can be defined as mountain, moor, heath, woodland, riverbank, beach or cliff. Technically speaking, hill goers who deviate from the designated paths, if there are any, are trespassing. This will vary from area to area. In the Lake District, however, above the intake walls, it is generally acknowledged that walkers and other outdoor users can wander just about anywhere without being accused of trespass – they have *de facto* access because of the length of time people have been venturing on to the fells. And similarly, in the Peak District there are access agreements with landowners for specified areas. These areas will be marked on the 1:25,000 scale maps. Mountain bikers have been known to be challenged by walkers who claim that it is only pedestrians who are included in these agreements. They can claim that mountain bikers, because they are relatively new to the outdoor scene, have no *de facto* rights of access. Actual permission from the landowners of open country areas can be gained but it must be stressed that mountain bikers cannot assume an automatic right to ride where they deem fit in open country. The local authority can supply information as to whether bikes are included within the ambit of the access agreements in a particular area. If not, cycling in the local hills may well be a trespass – bikers should bear this in mind when planning routes.

Many paths are open to bicycles.

The fun is to keep going right to the very top.

Deliberate and blatant trespass – accompanied with bad behaviour in particular – is not something that can be condoned. If you are unsure whether you are trespassing, go gently, be polite and make sure no other countryside users receive a bad impression about the way mountain bikers behave in public. Then check out the definitive map and if the way is marked as forbidden to access or if the landowner does not allow cyclists, then do not ride there again. To trespass willingly and to state this to be the plan of action to other mountain bikers makes you liable to the charge of conspiracy to trespass – this carries weighty penalties and although rarely enforced and hard to prove, it can mean large fines or even prison.

In Scotland the law of trespass is slightly different to the English system and is perhaps a little untidy – a fact Scottish mountain bikers and hill walkers usually use to their advantage. North of the border a landowner cannot sue for trespass unless he or she can prove actual damage has been done or that the trespass was for the purpose of hunting game. Walkers and mountain bikers are therefore unlikely to be challenged by landowners when they are either on paths or on terrain lacking in tracks. But still it is advisable to be as polite as possible if somebody asks you to leave the area you are cycling through. You are not necessarily obliged to leave but discretion is often the better part of valour – if you want to continue mountain biking in peace in that particular area again, it may be best to be diplomatic and accede to any demands issued to you. Rights of way in Scotland are not as well defined as in England and Wales and so, in effect, access is usually easier. This situation could change, however, if a court action ruled against a mountain biker – this could be taken as a precedent and Scottish bikers would then face very restricted access.

The following defines the various terms used when talking about rights of way and highways in England and Wales:

**Footpath**  As the name suggests a footpath is a right of way that allows access on foot only. In principle this is the case but technically speaking where there is a public right of way anybody, including cyclists, has the right to use the path as a linear route. This means that as long as the landowner concerned does not specifically object to bicycles or other 'carriages' (a bicycle is defined as a carriage in the Highway Act of 1980). There is no tested criminal law against cycling on a footpath.

Footpaths that run parallel to roads, however, are a different case. So, as it is stated in the Highway Act of 1980, it is illegal to ride on pavements (defined as a footway that runs parallel to a road). This is a criminal offence; riding on a footpath that avoids roads, is not – the landowner will have to sue for trespass. This state of affairs is complex and can lead to many arguments with fellow countryside users – so even though it may be allowable in some cases to cycle on footpaths it would be best to steer clear of them altogether. Some local councils have used their powers under the Local Government Act of 1972 (Section 235) to prohibit cyclists completely from footpaths. Therefore, where specific official signs on footpaths state that you should not cycle then you should obey them.

As the problem of bike access on footpaths is not clearly defined in law, mountain bikers must judge for themselves whether or not to cycle on them – discretion should be employed where necessary and both the rights of the landowner and the rights of fellow outdoor users must be taken into consideration. The characteristics of the path (is it wide enough for walkers and cyclists to pass in safety? Will it erode easily? Am I being a nuisance in using this path?) should all be evaluated. If in doubt find an alternative route – this time ensure it is wholly legal to be there. If a landowner can be persuaded to grant access to bikes then there will be no problem with riding on his paths. This is easier said than

Parkland paths are sometimes closed off to mountain bikers.

done however. Some people have managed it though, so there would be no harm in trying.

**Bridleway** This type of highway is the one most legally accessible to cyclists. In reality there is no specific common law right to access. However, under the Countryside Act of 1968 (Section 30) biking members of the public are granted the statutory right to ride their cycles on bridleways. One of the stipulations of this act is that cyclists should give way to walkers and horse riders – therefore although it is legal to ride on bridleways do not think you have the right to cycle past other countryside users at eighty miles per hour. This kind of behaviour is not exactly politic, so let horses and pedestrians have priority. Some fellow outdoor users however, may rant and rave at you even when you are completely in the right.

Some bridleways can also be closed to cyclists if the local authority so wishes. Signs have to be posted stipulating that no cycling is allowed and unlike trespass on private land which is a civil offence, riding on closed-off bridleways is a criminal offence and could end in prosecution.

Bridleways cannot be used for competitions – a fact often overlooked, or ignored, by many race organisers. Under no circumstances can permission be granted for any type of race that crosses, or uses, a bridleway; the same also applies to public footpaths. Under the rules of the 1972 Road Act a public highway, such as a road (or even a motorway!) can be closed off and used for racing – as long as the police and the Secretary for State grant permission, however, no one has the power to authorise a race on a bridleway. In the early days of mountain bike racing this rule was flaunted quite openly and nobody (except walkers with a sound knowledge of the law) seemed to mind. Today mountain biking is a high-profile sport and the 1972 Road Act rules are enforced more strongly. Certain races in 1989 crossed, and ran along, bridleways and this led to conflict between the race organisers and some local horse riders. The local horse riders were completely in the right. Apart from the risk of fights breaking out and the attendant risk of totally alienating fellow outdoor users, the use of bridleways for race-tracks would also lead to the race insurance becoming invalid in the eyes of the law. For obvious reasons this would be detrimental to the sport. It seems that the lessons have been learned however, and inadvertent use of bridleways in race circuits is now at an all time low. Racing on private land (either owned by independent landowners such as farmers, or by bodies such as the Forestry Commission) is fine so long as permission has been sought and granted in writing. However, where public rights of way cross this land racing is illegal.

Bridleways can be closed off to cycles by the imposition of Traffic Regulation Orders (TROs). These are a means whereby County and District Councils can effectively ban bicycles from the named bridleway section. TROs were originally created to halt bicycle traffic on bridleways that passed through new housing developments built on green field sites. The law, however, when it was formulated, was kept distinctly vague and local authorities can now use TROs as a means to ban bike traffic on any or all bridleways. When TROs are generated they are there for good – there is no known procedure for removing them. Certain high-use areas have TROs pending and this is either the result of over-zealous walkers and horse riders creating a fuss over the passage of dreaded mountain bikers, or the irresponsible and wild

behaviour of the bikers themselves – unfortunately it is often the fault of the latter. As I have previously stressed, and will keep on stressing, the great majority of mountain bikers are responsible people. It is such a shame that access may be restricted for us all because of the actions of a few.

**Roads Used as Public Paths** Otherwise known as RUPPs. A RUPP was originally defined as a highway, other than a public path, used by the public. RUPPs have a similar status to bridleways and cyclists have a statutory right to cycle there.

**Byways Open to All Traffic** The above definition of a RUPP was changed by the Wildlife and Countryside Act of 1981 (Section 53). So, RUPPs have usually been redesignated as Byways Open to All Traffic, or BOATs. Sometimes RUPPs can be downgraded at the whim of the local authority into footpaths, or moved sideways and redesignated as bridleways. BOATs allow all traffic, including vehicles, to pass. However where a RUPP has been redesignated as a footpath, the statutory right to ride a mountain bike, or any other cycle, no longer applies.

**Unclassified Country Roads** Also called UCRs, these are byways (usually unmetalled) and are open to all traffic. Bikes can ride on them at will. UCRs have to be maintained by the local authorities and they are classified on county highways maps (available for inspection at the local county hall). On the definitive map UCRs can be marked as byways, bridleways or even, in some cases as footpaths. The rights of way officer, if there is one, should be consulted as to the legal standing of, and access rights to, those local UCRs that appear on the definitive map as footpaths and the like. Ordnance Survey maps do not identify UCRs as such. Many UCRs may appear similar to farm roads and tracks so caution should be exercised when you come across a track or estate road on the map that does not have its status shown in full. Again

Unclassified country roads (UCRs) can be ridden upon at will.

if in doubt either steer clear altogether, or check your facts by spending a few hours in your local County Hall.

**Canal Tow-paths** These are flat and fairly boring for mountain bike use but they have the advantage of being linear routes that avoid busy roads. Their disadvantage lies in the fact that passage along them is usually very restricted. Most are owned by the British Waterways Board (BWB). The canal by-laws of the BWB prohibit cycling, however, permits are available as long as you can provide a good reason for travelling on a certain, specified stretch of tow-path and the cost of such permits is negligible. Tow-paths can also sometimes be classified as public rights of way although priority should always be given to the original and intended users of the tow-paths. Any tow-path that is not dedicated to the public is out of bounds. There is no statutory right of way and using them would be a trespass.

**Disused railway lines** Spotting an overgrown and totally disused old railway line (with the sleepers removed of course) is an exciting find. Chances are though that the route is out of bounds. Only those routes that have been cleared, resurfaced, way-marked and have been designated as cycle paths are permissible for you to cycle upon. There are many of these all around the country. There is a wonderful one on Tyneside which follows a meandering river and which has permissible paths coming off it at all angles with deep woodland on both sides. It is one of the closest and nicest routes available to me. The woods cover undulating ground and the rides here are never dull. Most areas in the country have similar routes.

**Forest tracks and paths** Permission will be required for riding through Forestry Commission land. Often this permission has already been granted by the local conservator and the Forestry Commission generally regards mountain biking favourably.

Other forests or woods will be privately owned and mountain biking is only permissible on the criteria listed above. Often there are very few rights of way going through woods and therefore technical trespass would be easy to commit.

The countryside, despite being well covered by rights of way can sometimes be closed off – that is, restrictions can legally be enforced in certain circumstances. These restrictions will, however, only be temporary. They should be adhered to very strictly indeed, otherwise the cause of mountain bike access could be damaged irreparably. There are often restrictions imposed when there is a high attendant fire risk on the hills, or when diseases such as foot-and-mouth break out. Rights of way can also be diverted if the local authority sees fit or if landowners have a good case for so doing.

Bikers should also take care in areas where lambing and other such agricultural and pastoral activities are taking place. At particularly sensitive times it may be prudent to avoid such areas altogether. The same might also apply when say an almost extinct plant has been given prominence by conservationists and the passage through conservation areas might cause either damage or disturbance. Mountain bikers should learn to be sympathetic to the ebbs and flows of the countryside. Even where we have distinct rights of way, access can sometimes be a delicate affair: be sensitive at all times; enjoy and respect the countryside; and absorb it rather than destroy it.

If a farmer or another landowner were to block off a legal right of way – or extinguish it in any other way, (for instance by ploughing a field where you know there to be a highway) and the landowner does not restore the path within three weeks, then contact your local authority and complain. If the path is well used then your local ramblers will already be on red-alert. Try to project a caring image – reason with the landowner and explain that the passage of mountain bikes will do his livelihood no harm. If all else fails and you know the route to be a definite and well-used right of way feel free to make the path again by cycling along and trampling the ground back. If there are crops growing trample them down and if barbed wire keeps you out cut it down – but you must make sure this is a right of way and is open to cyclists. If you do not fancy being quite so much of an anarchist then instead complain further to your local authority and possibly get the backing of the Mountain Bike Club.

All the above definitions and restrictions may seem fairly Draconian but bear in mind that there are thousands of miles of routes that are totally open to the passage of fat-tyres and conflicts with fellow outdoor users need not come about.

As a result of the increased leisure time of an expanded population, the enhanced mobility cars give us, the higher standard of living most of us enjoy and the growth of outdoor activities within education, the hills have never been busier. Many competing outdoor activities vie for the same space. However, it is not simply recreation that the countryside is used for. Indeed, it is not as much of a playground as some people would like to believe. Hill and mountain country, as well as agricultural lowland, is productive land – in one form or another. Many people make their livelihoods from it. Forestry, agriculture, tourism, sporting activities, water gathering, mineral exploitation, power generation and military training all take place in the countryside. Clearly many of these activities are not compatible with each other, and so fitting mountain biking into an already crowded picture is not an easy task.

As a consequence of the greatly increased numbers of people who want to get into the great outdoors to play – whether it be by bike, canoe, foot, or hang-glider – restrictions may have to be imposed on all countryside users. The south of England may not be much affected by such changes but certainly hill country looks likely to be affected in a big way. National parks and other such domains may start banning mountain bikers for reasons of safety and to lessen the risk of erosion. Alternatively permits may have to be purchased to gain entry on to land that up until now has been free. However, such payment for use of the hills will not just have to be borne by mountain bikers – all users may have to end up paying for their outdoor recreations.

Specific ATB tracks may be set aside and devoted wholly to mountain bike usage. Walkers may get similar deals. In the Viewpoints section later on in this chapter, Max Glaskin of the Mountain Bike Club explains how the Forestry Commission is starting to think about zoning off parts of its land to enable segregation of walkers, cross-country skiers and mountain bikers. Given that the use of the countryside for leisure purposes will continue to grow, these types of changes will undoubtedly become more widespread.

For mountain bikers to get a good deal when these changes come about, the attitudes of many will have to alter radically. Responsibility towards the countryside, its fellow users and the landowners will be a major factor in deciding whether we continue to have a lively off-road sport or instead if we find ourselves getting banned completely. Huge tracts of land have been closed off to mountain bikers in America. With luck, and with the efforts of such campaigning bodies as the MBC, the same will not happen here.

Mountain bikers should try to adhere to the following three codes of practice issued by the Countryside Commission, the Forestry Commission and the Mountain Bike Club respectively:

## The Country Code

Enjoy the countryside and respect its life and work.
Guard against all risk of fire.
Fasten all gates.
Keep your dogs under close control.
Keep to rights of way across farmland.
Use gates and stiles to cross fences, hedges and walls.
Leave livestock, crops and machinery alone.
Take your litter home.
Help to keep all water clean.
Protect wildlife, plants and trees.
Take special care on country roads.
Make no unnecessary noise.

## The Forest Code and the Forest Bicycling Code

Observe the Highway Code riding rules.
Make sure your cycle is safe to ride and is prepared for difficult conditions.
Ride slowly and not more than two abreast.
Give way to vehicles and walkers.
Take care in skiddy conditions.
Do not ride after dark.
Guard against all fire risks.
Leave things as you find them. Take nothing away.
Do not leave open or obstruct gates and, for your own safety, keep clear of forest operations. Respect the work of the forest.
Camp only on approved land.
Obtain permission when required.
Respect the peace and quiet of the forest and avoid disturbing others.

## The Off-road Code

Only ride where you know you have a legal right.
Always yield to horses and to pedestrians.
Avoid animals and crops. In some cir-cumstances this may not be possible, at which times contact should be kept to a minimum.
Take all litter with you.
Leave all gates as found.
Keep the noise down.
Do not get annoyed with anyone, it never solves any problems.
Always try to be self-sufficient, for you and your bike.
Never create a fire hazard.

# Viewpoints

*What can be done about the various access problems now happening to mountain biking in this country?*

**Max Glaskin** 'Well, that is down to education. Because we live in a car-orientated society people often do not know how to act in the countryside. The Sports Council and the Countryside Commission are doing their bit at education by publishing the Mountain Bike Code, which covers most of the salient points. It is a case of reaching the people who know nothing about the countryside and how to behave in it. If everybody knew how to behave in the countryside on a bicycle – and knew what to do and what not to do – there would be no problem with access. On the whole 98 per cent of the people would obey the written, and the unwritten, laws.

In no way could we advocate any confrontations with landowners – mountain bikers are new to the scene, feet have been round longer. Mountain bikes have no automatic right to the countryside. By pure chance they can use certain rights of way – bridlepaths and BOATs for example, for which those highways were not initially dedicated to. So I think the important thing is to protect these rights. There are areas where mountain bikes have been deliberately excluded from bridleways through the local by-laws – we have to make sure this does not happen anywhere else and we should realise that landowners have various priorities but they are also only human and should be talked to.

Large landowners such as the Forestry Commission have been wonderful so far. In fact we are now discussing with the Forestry Commission the possibilities of zoning various forests, purely for the use of mountain bikers to the exclusion of all other users – and this is under serious consideration, particularly for some of the larger forests in Scotland. All of which is really good news for us – and not necessarily bad news for the other countryside users because they are also to get exclusive zones. It is to prevent conflict. The access problems we have now are only due to lack of education on the part of mountain bikers. They have got to learn as quickly as possible otherwise they will get themselves thrown off the land – and they will only have themselves to blame.

I have no sympathy for anybody who starts trespassing and then tells the farmer to get lost. Mountain bikers have a duty to the countryside and to the people who make a living from it. If they perform that duty there will be no conflict. I do not want to sound too authoritarian but we are in an extremely vulnerable position.'

*Given the access problems in the States do you think we have anything to learn from the American situation?*

**Mike Kloser** 'Well, the real problems are in the over-populated areas and where there is high-use of the land. On the public-use lands – where you have people hiking and horse riding – people are often offended by all the cyclists but off-road cyclists have nowhere to go but on the already existing trails and roads. Yet they are being fined, ticketed, there are radar-guns on the trails, there are signs telling you not to go over fifteen miles per hour on descents – it is really bad. Lots of trails are being shut down altogether. So what needs to be done is more like what happens in Colorado – the forests are multi-use so they are very open to mountain bikers and there is really not so much conflict. Also we need to form more trail access groups that can work to keep mountain bike trails open. It is not just an individual effort that is going to safeguard trails – it has got to be a group effort and it has got to be mutually agreed upon with the hikers and the horse riders. Everybody has got to have their guide-lines to go by. They are going to have to be followed in the over-populated areas otherwise it is not going to work. Obviously there is a conflict – but it is an awareness programme problem, and if everybody can put their heads together instead of being so selfish I think it will work out.'

*Have you noticed that mountain bikers are less caring about the environment than say walkers or other outdoor users?*

**Arthur Phillips** 'There is an irresponsible element in any population using the hills. Mountain bikers are no exception and the sport is bringing to the hills a new group of people, some of whom see the countryside only as a free race-track for ATBs. This element is going to give us a lot of trouble, since one of their favourite sports is frightening the wits out of parties of staid, and maybe elderly, ramblers, most of whom are probably members of the Ramblers Association.'

# 4 The Mountain Biker's Wardrobe

(Clothe Thyself)

The original Californian 'clunker riders' had a distinct way of dressing – both men and women would sport blue jeans, a woollen check lumberjack shirt, a baseball cap and a pair of leather gloves; and if it was cold a down body-warmer. For Californian dirt hillsides this set-up is fine – and especially so for protection from crashes. It is basically the wardrobe of a typical American back-woodsman. In Britain this garb would be seen as somewhat eccentric by the modern mountain biker – yet apart from the jeans, this gear is quite practical. It is hard-wearing and with the addition of a windproof shell garment and some form of quick-drying, windproof legwear it could easily be adapted for mountain biking in the UK.

Road-racing clothes are popular with mountain bikers.

However, it is the kind of clothing as favoured by out-and-out road racing cyclists that is fast becoming the norm for modern mountain bikers. In defence of cycle clothing it must be said that Lycra skin shorts are the most practical items of legwear available – at least as long as the weather is not too cold and if you do not mind having your legs cut up from thorns and the odd crash or two. Ron Hill Tracksters are good long protective legwear and come in exotic colours; alternatively Lycra tights can be worn. Wearing Lycra anywhere other than your legs is, however, extremely impractical. In winter and in summer if venturing into the hills, we should therefore follow the lead of other serious outdoor users and adopt clothes designed for use in inclement conditions. The American back woodsman set-up would now

seem quite dated considering the advances in 'outdoor' fabrics, so it is the modern outdoor activists that we must learn from.

Many mountain bikers have come into the sport via some other outdoor activity. Ramblers and backpackers enjoy the speed of quickly biking across the kind of terrain that would take them ten times as long to cover by hiking; and climbers recognise that using an all-terrain bike to transport them to the crags is far easier than slogging along on foot. The type of outdoor apparel these converts to mountain biking wear when out on the bike is the same sort of clothing they would use in their parallel activities. In other words sensible clothing made for serious outdoor use.

Many mountain bikers do, however, still prefer Lycra as their sole protection from the

Lycra looks fantastic but may not be good hill wear.

Polycotton windproofs are good for cycling in.

Many mountain bikers have come into the sport via some other outdoor activity.

elements. This wonder material may be light-weight, skin-tight and showy, but for practical-ity it scores a zero. On its own, or in a nylon mix, Lycra is a poor outdoor material, although it must be admitted that when it is included in a polycotton mix it acts as a shaping agent and garments made from this cease to be quite so impractical. Being clad in fluorescent nylon-Lycra garments on the streets or on safe, low-level bridlepaths is fine – they look good and chances are you are never too far away from shelter and warmth should there be a sudden change in the weather. The fact that Lycra gets damp and sticky from perspiration is again not too much of a problem if you are only travelling for a few commuter-minutes. When you trans-late this material to the hills however, and add a few choice weather conditions it is then that nylon-based materials begin to lose their appeal.

Considering their highly energetic activities road racing cyclists insist on wearing the most absurd of materials. Serious outdoor users have known for years the kind of clothes that should be worn to be comfortable in a range of temper-atures and to be protected from the vagaries of the British climate – Lycra is certainly not on their list of sensible materials. The kind of garb racing cyclists often wear is ineffective for the streets, never mind the hills. Huge advances have been made in fibre origination and the like yet still the cyclist wears clothes more suited to the disco dance-floor than the great outdoors. Modern materials though, are not dull and life-less; no longer do they come in just greens and browns – indeed they can be made just as 'jazzy' as Lycra. For instance, some of the new fabrics can now accept sublimated 'prints' rather than dyes, so some exotically designed polycotton, or polyester, cycling tops are becoming avail-able for those cyclists who above all want to be comfortable, but want to be noticed at the same time! Bright colours may cause raised eyebrows from some quarters, but certainly from the visibility and safety aspect, a cyclist who wears fluorescent pink is at least going to be seen – some of the bright clothing is there-fore also functional.

Racing mountain bikers, who compete regu-larly, usually wear road racing clothes – in other words skin tops and shorts. For low-level com-petitions this kind of gear is fine. For the really mountainous courses – now quite rare, if not extinct – racers should at least throw out the Lycra and put on a polycotton cycling top instead. If the race is a lengthy one a lightweight windproof – which can weigh next to nothing – should be tucked in a small saddle bag along with a basic tool-kit and some energy food. If a racer gets round the whole course these extras will not be needed, but if he or she has a crash miles from the next check-point, or if the bike breaks down, then he or she will be slightly more able to withstand a possible deterioration in the weather.

Many companies now manufacture 'jazzy' cycle clothing that is made out of good material. If you want to be comfortable and look like a cyclist then choose tops made out of polyesters and cotton – a fifty/fifty mix is best. These will fold up small, will be fairly wear-resistant and will dry quickly. This fast drying ability is a very important consideration – mind you one hundred per cent polyester garments will also dry rapidly, but they do not have as many advan-tages as polycotton. Much of the Fast Italia and Been Bag clothing is made from a mix of poly-ester and cotton, as is some of the excellent Swallow range. The Been Bag Viloft material (65 per cent polyester, 35 per cent viscose) is also very good – the material's interior loop-pile stitching draws sweat away very well and the garments keep their tight figure-hugging shape long after their first trip out. The face does tend to pill however (pilling is the balling of the polyester – when tiny bobbles appear on the exterior of the material and is a common problem with such synthetic fabrics as fleeces, pile fabrics and so forth).

The best mountain jackets.

The extreme exertion of cycling, compared to say walking, coupled with regular stops – either for catching your breath, admiring the view, or both – means the cyclist's clothing ensemble has a pretty hard job to perform. Maintaining a constant temperature with all of these starts and stops is difficult. One minute you are literally steaming up a hill and then the next your sweat is evaporating instantly during a downhill section; an impromptu stop will then mean even more evaporation and before you know it you are shivering. If you choose the right clothes and wear them in the right way then you can, however, eliminate this tendency towards excessive heat loss and can prevent possible exposure cases.

The basic principles behind dressing for outdoor activities are firstly that clothes should be made of the right materials; secondly they should fit well so as to allow adequate movement, but should not be so loose as to flap about in gusts of wind (this would lead to excessive skin cooling and the creation of unnecessary wind resistance); thirdly they should pack down into as little a volume as possible, so that carrying them is no great problem; fourthly they should lose little insulating value when wet; and finally they should be worn in layers. Underwear made of the right materials should absorb sweat, or draw (wick) it away from the skin, quickly and efficiently so as to prevent excessive cooling and thereby maintain a constant, normal body temperature. The middle and outer garments should allow this water vapour to pass unhindered and should keep the wearer warm from within and shielded from

Mountain bike clothing should fit well.

wind and rain from the outside. If the weather is fine just the underwear can be worn (although even when it is warm you should take care that your body's microclimate, or layer of air insulation, is safeguarded, so always try to avoid wind-permeable clothes). If it starts to rain the outer garment can be put on and if the temperature drops radically then the middle garments can be added. If the weather is being particularly nasty then other mid-layers can be worn (for instance thin polyester-fleece tops or woolly jumpers) and then removed as the cyclist heats up. Layers should be added again when the cyclist stops for a break – a constant temperature can therefore be maintained. This layering principle is standard advice for hill walkers and other outdoor users; it should also be standard advice for mountain bikers venturing away from the city streets.

Even on the streets, however, you do not

Hill apparel can be worn in the city too.

want to be constantly uncomfortable because of any ill-considered choice of commuter cycling garb and so hill apparel can be worn in the city too. I personally have not worn 'ordinary' clothing when riding on the streets for years – jeans constrict the leg muscles too much and cotton T-shirts soak up sweat and do not dry out easily. Most of the time, therefore, I wear windproof polycotton Rohan trousers; synthetic, or silk, T-shirts that draw sweat away; windproof mid-layers such as a Rohan polycotton Moving-On (or if it is cold, a fleece jacket or jumper such as the Mountain Equipment Ultra-fleece); and to top it off, if needed, a waterproof jacket made from Gore-Tex or one of the other breathable materials. If it is not forecast for heavy rain then a lightweight polycotton or microfibre jacket can be worn instead. My favourite wind and showerproof microfibre shell garment is the Climaguard one made by Karrimor. This lets sweat out admirably (unlike Gore-Tex which is comparatively slow at pumping out the perspiration), blocks the wind totally and is lightweight and stylish. At least if I get caught in a shower when out commuting I know that I can step from the bike and be bone dry within about twenty minutes. Body heat dries out these materials quite quickly but if you sit in a warm room you will dry even faster – that is if you do not mind people staring at your steaming clothes! For commuting this kind of clothing is great – the cut on most of these garments is generous to facilitate energetic movements and they are all hardwearing. When layered effectively they can be comfortable across a huge range of temperatures and conditions.

What is good for the city, comfortwise, can be a life-saver on the hills. Setting out in the morning with the promise of a glorious day of sunshine ahead might lead your average mountain biker to leave the middle and outer wear garments behind. But it is common knowledge that heading off with only a pair of shorts,

Rohan windproof tops.

A waterproof jacket is a must.

a T-shirt and some day-glo sunglasses is not a sensible way to go about an outdoor activity especially in the hills. Getting caught out in a protracted mountain downpour is not funny if all you have on your back is a sodden T-shirt and all you are carrying is a near-empty rucksack and a couple of damp sandwiches, but no foul-weather clothing.

Mountain bikers do, on the whole, venture into the hills with common sense as far as dress is concerned, but still many's the time when in-experienced ATBers have ventured that little bit too far with a noticeable lack of adequate outdoor clothing and safety equipment. Mountain rescue teams can attest to this. Mountain biking does generate a lot of heat however, so as long as a stricken ATBer can keep pedalling he or she should at least get down the hills safely – although not in comfort.

Weather descends rapidly in the UK and none faster than hill weather. A bank of clouds can travel far quicker than you can cycle and even if you saw a rainstorm approaching you generally would not have time to get very far off the hills before it hit.

What kind of clothing – specific mountain clothing – should you wear to be protected against the British climate? It is all a matter of taste – some people will prefer the traditional garments made out of wool, silk and cotton; others will go for the latest in high-tech lami-nates, polyester derivatives and tight loom-spun nylons. When choosing which to go for, price can be one good decider – for the new synthetics it can safely be stated that they do not come cheap. A Gore-Tex shell garment (for example, a model from the Berghaus Extrem range) with features galore and colours to match will set the mountain biker back nearly a couple of hundred pounds – half a decent bike in other words! Similarly a flashy fleece jumper can cost upwards of seventy pounds (for example a Mountain Equipment Kashmira). A woolly jumper and a cotton wind breaker on the

other hand could both be picked up at an army surplus store for less than twenty pounds – although they would not be as effective as the synthetic garments. Therefore, generally speaking, the synthetics are by far the more expensive.

Synthetics are in vogue at the moment and such long-sleeved tops as the Helly-Hansen Lifa polyprop ones are all but ubiquitous on the hills. More traditional materials may come back into fashion but at the moment they do not have as large a market share as the synthetics. This is a shame because for some of their wear characteristics, wool and silk garments can be just as good as many of their man-made rivals. Although speaking personally, I think Capilene, a permanently-treated polyester, would seem to be the best choice overall for underwear; fleece the best choice for mid-wear; and Gore-Tex and Sympatex the best choices for shell garments – this will be discussed further later in the chapter.

First we must learn about the dynamics of the human body and its microclimate when at rest and when exercising. At all times the inner core of the body (the trunk section where all the major organs are situated) must be kept at a temperature of 37°C. If the body is cold, involuntary actions such as shivering and the appearance of goosebumps will aim to conserve this core temperature. If, on the other hand, the body begins to overheat then we start to sweat thus losing the heat through evaporation of the sweat. Heat is also lost by convection (such a heat loss occurs when air comes into contact with the body or clothing and then moves away carrying some of the body heat with it); by radiant heat loss (this loss occurs from solid to solid without the air around being warmed, in a similar fashion to the way the sun heats the earth); and by conduction if you are mountain biking in the snow and sit down on an icy patch!

As mountain biking involves working up a

sweat the garments we wear should control the amount of sweat that evaporates directly from the skin when we stop for a rest. We actually perspire all the time – not just when we start to exercise. When at rest, insensible perspiration occurs – this is a water vapour loss from the epidermis (the stratified outer layers of mammalian skin) and not the sweat glands. It does not regulate temperature to any great degree (except in cold and dry conditions) but is thought to be associated with the growth and ageing process of the lower skin cells as they form keratin (the component of skin, hair and nails). It also prevents the skin from drying out and cracking. The average adult loses about five hundred grams of water through insensible perspiration every twenty-four hours – so wearing impermeable plastic cagoules would be unbearable at rest as well as at play!

When we start to generate too much heat the sweat glands are activated and they begin to secrete water as a liquid on to the skin so it can evaporate and cool us down – this is called sensible perspiration. This second form of perspiration wets clothes easily. Therefore when we come to a rest (bearing in mind that chilling will occur with wet clothing next to the skin) underwear needs to be able to absorb sweat. Wool can absorb up to 30 per cent of its own weight in water and still feel dry. Above this level of moisture retention wool becomes saturated and will take a long time to dry. Alternatively underwear must be able to transport sweat away from the skin – such as treated polyester materials which draw (or 'wick') the moisture away. Materials should also be highly 'breathable' so as to allow the vapour component of sweat to escape. Wool underwear (for instance the soft Best range) is slightly more breathable than synthetic materials. Breathable middle and outer layers are also necessary to prevent the vapour condensing on the inside of the garments.

# TYPES OF FABRIC

## Underwear

**Wool**   A warm keratin-based material that is a good sweat absorber. Wool, thanks partly to its high content of air spaces, is a relatively poor conductor and so can slow down the rate at which we lose heat to our surrounding environment. The natural springiness of wool (its 'crimp'), the tiny surface fibres and the scales on the fibres, trap still air which prevents body heat from escaping. Wool hygroscopically absorbs moisture (takes moisture up) unlike polyester which is hydrophilic and 'gets rid' of moisture by transporting it elsewhere. It feels dry to the touch and therefore warm – even when it is wet as it has the ability to store moisture away from its surface. However, as stated before, once saturated it becomes wet to the touch and will take a very long time to dry.

Unlike certain synthetic materials wool does not magnify body odours and can be worn for lengthy periods if absolutely necessary. It should, however, be cleaned regularly if performance is to be maintained. A matted and greasy woollen jumper will be less efficient because the fibres are packed down. Although, in saying this, it must be realised that frequent washing will strip the wool of natural oils, and therefore the woollen garments will not shed water quite so easily as they did when new. Some people hate wool next to the skin but the new softer yarns now available (for instance from Baselayer or Best) do not have a tendency to itch or irritate. For winter mountain biking wool undershirts are a good idea, but try not to fall in any rivers when wearing them and make sure you ventilate them well beneath other layers as they can be very warm.

**Silk**   Knitted silk thermal undergarments have been popular for centuries. Even World War II fighter pilots used to wear silk beneath their flying suits in order to keep them warm.

Silk is strong, lightweight, absorbent, warm and feels nice next to the skin. After washing, a 'lived-in' patina or sheen develops which does not destroy silk's many properties. It has a low heat conductivity and so again is a good insulator; like wool it can absorb up to thirty per cent of its weight in moisture whilst still feeling dry; it becomes a second skin if worn snugly (all underwear should be worn snugly); it has a lower density and weight per square centimetre than wool, cotton and some synthetics; it is flexible and stretches well; and again, like wool, it can absorb the bacteria that lead to body odour smells on garments. It works well in both summer and winter but one of its main disadvantages is that most types of silk should be hand-washed and dried flat. However, the new Thermasilk range made in China, but imported from America, can be machine-washed and hung up to dry. My Survival Aids silk top however, has always been washed 'badly' and it still functions perfectly. Survival Aids produce a wide range of silk garments including T-shirts, long-sleeved vests, long johns, socks, glove liners and Balaclavas. The 'headover' – a silk tube made for wearing around the neck is especially useful. In deserts I use it as a face-mask – being see-through I do not need goggles when sandstorms hit!

**Cotton** This is a comfortable material for underwear if you are not going to be doing anything strenuous. But for active sports, such as mountain biking, T-shirts made from cotton are not a good idea. Unless, that is, they have polyester added to them, which will aid drying times. It wicks well but once it gets hold of it, it tends to hang on to water. Cotton will feel clammy next to the skin after just a short time on the bike and it feels very cold when wet – this could rapidly take away valuable body heat. Cottons are good for hot climate pedalling but for Britain it is best to keep designer T-shirts for the city streets. Do not take them on to the hills; polycotton T-shirts are good though.

**Synthetics** These are now very popular with outdoor users despite their very obvious disadvantages. The synthetics developed for active outdoor use are all good wicking agents and, if worn snugly, will keep a layer of insulating air next to the skin. They also dry rapidly, but some of them do start to smell quite quickly. Natural body oils block the fabric up and many synthetics cease to function properly if not washed regularly. This point is not important for those mountain bikers who have easy access to an automatic washing machine but for long-distance tourers, water is possibly going to be scarce and regular laundry stops may not be possible. Synthetic underwear (except for Capilene and Dunova), therefore, is not the best thing to take on extended, wilderness tours. Some synthetics also need to be carefully washed and dried as excessive heat will melt, distort or shrink them. Remember that some only wick because of a surface chemical treatment which will wash out eventually. Capilene, chlorofibre, Dunova, Dryline and polypropylene are the most readily available synthetics.

Capilene is a treated polyester fabric and is the best in practical terms. Usually polyester is hydrophobic (water-repelling) but the surface of Capilene fibres have been chemically altered to make them hydrophilic (water-attracting). Therefore the outer skin of a Capilene fibre absorbs water, while the inner, untreated core, repels it – this produces a fabric that mechanically transports water by wicking. Through a 'spreading action' the fibres draw moisture from wet areas and transport them to drier ones where the moisture spreads out and evaporates. This is an unusual wicking mechanism – in the other wickable fabrics it is capillary action and vapour transmission that draws the moisture through the fabric. The former mechanism is where the movement of moisture is between interlocked fibres and the latter is the direct passage of water vapour through the open weave of a non-absorbent fabric.

The makers of Capilene claim that it removes moisture from the skin more readily than any other material. Heady claims indeed and in practice hard to prove but certainly Capilene is a fabric (which comes in three weights for different uses) which works well when you are physically working hard. Capilene is also more indestructible than the other synthetics – it can take repeated washings and is not affected by tumble-drying. As you may have surmised it is my favourite fabric for wearing during action sports.

Chlorofibre, from such companies as North Cape or Damart, is often mixed with other fibres such as Modal (a derivative of beechwood). It has a very soft feel, wicks well and dries quite quickly. After washing in warm water though it cannot be left on radiators or tumble-dried as it shrinks and melts when heat is applied. It retains body odours but for single day sorties into the wilds it is comfortable and practical.

One of the better synthetics is Dunova, as once sold by Rohan. It can still be found, in a different form, if you check the labels on 'thermal' underwear in high street shops. When it was available in the Rohan design it wicked superbly and kept the wearer dry even under the severest of exertions. It is an acrylic fibre that has an inner absorbant fibre which is surrounded by a non-absorbent, porous sheath. Moisture is wicked from the surface of the skin by capillary action. Today's versions normally include a mix of other synthetics, or cotton, as well and so it does not work quite as well, but, if you are lucky, a one hundred per cent Dunova garment can sometimes be discovered in obscure mens outfitters. Many people believe Dunova, made by Bayer of Germany, was the best of all the synthetics – except perhaps Capilene. Rohan withdrew it because supplies, for some strange reason, just dried up. Rohan then switched to a Dryline material for their underwear range. This was a one hundred per

cent knitted polyester fabric that has also since been discontinued although Dryline T-majors and T-minors can sometimes be bought very cheaply at Rohan sales. These T's were made into two-layer garments with just one 'mesh' layer under the arms and as a side panel. The loosely knitted inner mesh layer transports sweat away to the denser knit exterior so dry air is maintained next to the skin. Garments made from Dryline look very good, even as street wear (the T-major had a zipped pouch pocket on the front) and work extremely well. They resist pilling and if it is not too breezy can be worn as an exterior garment with ease.

Polypropylene (also known as Meraklon) is a popular synthetic undergarment. It may be popular, but it certainly is not the best. The Helly-Hansen Lifa fabric pills terribly and it does not remain effective for as long as some of the other fabrics. Helly-Hansen to their credit came up with an improvement to their Lifa garment. They developed a new polypropylene fabric that can be worn effectively for longer periods, which is much more heat-resistant and which should therefore have a more extended life.

## Design Features to Look out for

Underwear made from any of the materials above – whether natural fabrics or man-made fabrics – will perform much better than 'ordinary' clothing when translated to a mountain biking situation. However, there are certain features you should check when you are selecting such garments: underwear should be very snug fitting; long sleeves are more versatile than short; zipped polo necks could be a better choice than plain collars as they can be rolled up or down as conditions dictate – thereby allowing more efficient ventilation; the upper garment should be long enough to cover the kidney area with plenty of room to spare; because of mountain biking's tendency for extreme exertions the lightest weight 'thermals' should be chosen – often medium and thick versions are available of the same garments but cost more and do not perform as well – vapour transmission is restricted in heavier garments and should only be worn by walkers and the like in very cold conditions.

# Mid-wear Layers

Insulating layers can be made up from filled garments such as body-warmers (stuffed with duck down or synthetic fillers). These will generally be too warm for active mountain biking (although a lightweight down vest can be packed into a very small space and could be useful for donning when at rest) and so the mid-wear layers most suited to mountain biking are wool, polycotton or the polyester fleeces and piles.

**Wool** This is an effective middle garment material which breathes well. Because the interlocking fibres trap air, its insulation capabilities are excellent, and, as stated above, so long as it does not get very wet it will keep the wearer warm and cosy. It can still be warm when wet though. Weight for weight it is not as efficient as some of the synthetic insulating layers, but everybody has at least one woolly jumper knocking around so there is not really any need to go to the expense of buying fleece pullovers or jackets (unless you really want to).

**Polycotton** Many popular sweatshirts are made out of a fifty/fifty mix of polyester and cotton and so would be usable as mid-layer wear in cool, dry conditions. Once wet they are cold, heavy and are slow drying. Windproof polycotton tops as manufactured by various companies are surprisingly warm when worn over a thermal undergarment. This is because the tightly-woven thread (either a mixed thread or two separate threads – one polyester, one cotton) blocks wind well. On most days of the year, even in winter, all that will be needed is just such a combination. A Rohan Moving-On

can be donned over a Capilene top or a polycotton cycling top and will keep out the wind and any light showers very well. When you start to warm up the neck closure can be opened and the sleeves rolled up. For strenuous uphills, sudden downhills and the starting and stopping of an average sortie into the outdoors this two-layer outfit is perfect. As long as a shell garment is also carried, and maybe a warm lightweight item, this can form the year-round mountain biking wardrobe.

**Fleece and pile** As mentioned above fleeces and piles are warmer weight for weight than wool. They also dry more quickly, absorb hardly any moisture and keep much of their loft when damp (their warm air pockets). Fleeces and piles can be made out of either polyester or nylon. Most are polyester. They are extremely hard-wearing and except for pilling (which is not so prevalent in modern fleeces) garments made from such fluffy fabrics can look brand-new many months after purchase.

Whilst the terms pile and fleece are now almost interchangeable the generally accepted way of differentiating between the two is to check the feel of the garment. Fleece has a smooth, brushed finish, is tightly woven and is therefore partly wind-resistant. Pile fabrics are loosely woven, extremely wind-permeable, tend to be more furry and are rougher to the touch. Manufacturers of such garments cannot decide between themselves how to classify the material types they are working with. Thus, Polarplus – made by the American firm Malden Mills, from Dacron Du Pont polyester – is called fleece by Karrimor and yet Malden Mills still call it pile. There are also various trade names that different manufacturers stick on their fleeces and piles – what is Polarplus to one manufacturer can be called Synchilla by another (Patagonia).

The thick fleeces and piles are too warm for anything other than sedentary mountain biking. The lightweight fleeces such as Mountain Equipment's Ultrafleece or Malden Mills' Polarlite (as made up into garments by various manufacturers) are the best for mountain biking. The Ultrafleece jumpers or jackets can act as outer garments if it is not too windy; and when the weather is harsh they can be worn under a shell garment without becoming unbearably warm. Most of the other fleeces and piles need to be covered by windproofs because their open weave lets wind through easily.

## Design Features to Look out for

Mid-layers come in a variety of styles all of which have their benefits and drawbacks. A woolly jumper – the simplest mid-layer – has no extra design features but is cheap and a few thin ones can be worn, or carried, thereby multiplying the effective air insulation (air trapped between the layers will account for about thirty per cent of the total insulation). A fleece or pile smock can control temperature remarkably despite its over-the-head design. Mid-layer garments should have closures at the neck to prevent warm air escaping and to assist in ventilation when necessary. Jackets with full-length zips are probably the easiest to ventilate and can be a good all-round choice; they also have higher necks which can keep the neck warm and shield it from the wind. When choosing a fleece or pile garment make sure it is designed for hill use rather than for city streets. A hill garment will not have knitted stretch cuffs or hems – these absorb moisture, retain it and feel very cold when wet – but will have thin Lycra ones. Nylon fronted middle layer fleeces are available but not versatile enough for mountain biking. The Pertex-fronted Buffalo Mountain shirt is a bulky, warm garment good for people who really feel the cold and for desperate conditions; it is, however, too warm for most biking days. Choose the lightweight fleeces every time and carry more than one if necessary.

Mid-wear can be made water-resistant if it is

washed in such proofing agents as TX-10 – a fleece jumper or a polycotton top can be made very weatherproof in this way. Do remember to treat proofed garments differently from non-proofed ones. When laundering make sure the proofed garments are washed with a mild detergent, otherwise the proofing will be gradually stripped away. Nikwax, who make TX-10 and Texnik (which can waterproof maps as well as tents), also make Loft – a specialist detergent formulated for washing proofed garments.

# Outer Layers

Shell garments should preferably be waterproof and breathable. On some days you can risk just taking a windproof shell garment, although it would be best to don the windproof and still have a further waterproof in your rucksack. It should be stressed that any manufacturer who claims a garment is one hundred per cent waterproof is telling lies: water can seep in at the seams as not every seam can be taped and sealed; hood and cuff opening areas will let some amounts of rain in; water can be wicked up from the base of sleeves; and under extreme conditions rain can penetrate the baffles in front of zips. Some shell garments are more water-resistant than others, but nothing could ever be claimed to be fully waterproof. Manufacturers claim their *material* is waterproof – this is not necessarily a lie – but *garments* are not.

There are no standard or legal definitions of 'water-resistant', 'shower-resistant', 'water-repellent' or 'breathable' (one for this is imminent) – some manufacturers use them interchangeably and this can be misleading. Berghaus, a much respected outdoor clothing manufacturer, uses the following definitions for their fabrics:

**Water-resistant** This is measured in centimetres of hydrostatic head (water entry pressure). To be water-resistant a fabric needs to have a minimum hydrostatic head of 100cm.

Keep spare clothing, energy food and emergency gear in a small volume
rucksack.

**Showerproof** This is any fabric that has a hydrostatic head lower than 100cm but has had its surface treated for water repellancy.

**Water-repellent** This is when a fabric's outer surface is treated with a durable water repellent (DWR) finish, making water skim off its surface. It helps the shedding properties of a fabric but often does not last the full life of a garment – garments can often be reproofed however.

There is, however, a British Standard for the definition of 'waterproof'. This standard is set at a hydrostatic head of 150cm. Berghaus sets its own standard to be 200cm.

It should be noted that the weakest part of any shell garment is at the seams and it is not uncommon for untaped, or badly taped, seams to have entry pressures of only about 10–20cm – you should therefore choose garments that have as few seams as possible. Multi-coloured jackets that look good in the city may well have a multitude of seams and despite being made from the most high-tech of fabrics they may leak like sieves! However, high-quality technical, or specialist, manufacturers should have no problem taping seams well. In fact many Sympatex and Gore-Tex garments, from respected manufacturers, have taped seams with higher hydrostatic heads than the main material!

Gore-Tex is the market leader in waterproof shell garments and has been since the mid-1970s. Because of its highly technical nature it is also expensive. The fabric is, of course, 'breathable' but sweat will still condense on its inner surface if the exertion, or the metabolic rate of the wearer, is high. The same is true of all the synthetic breathables – even the micro-fibre ones. Gore-Tex, the material, comes in a number of weights (layers of polyester or nylon and Gore-Tex lamination), the heavier of which are more durable, but also more unwieldy. The two-layer construction material will breathe better than the three-layer one. Gore-Tex itself is an expanded PTFE membrane (which stands for polytetrafluoroethylene!), which in turn is protected on one or both sides by another fabric. In its time it was quite a unique concept and caused a revolution in outdoor fabrics. It spawned many imitators but only Sympatex, from the German firm Akzo (formerly Enka), has ever really equalled its breathability.

Gore-Tex works because of its thousands of perforations – water as vapour, being so microscopic in size, can pass out through the microporous membrane (also called a poromeric membrane). There are, in fact, nine billion 'pores' per square inch. As water vapour molecules are seventy times smaller than one of these pores they can be pumped out through the membrane easily. The pores also happen to be misaligned, microscopically of course, and therefore wind cannot penetrate the fabric. Liquid water cannot penetrate the fabric either as raindrops are far too big to be able to dig their way through the pores. It is only on untaped seams and other stitching points that water can penetrate.

Gore-Tex and other microporous fabrics need to be kept clean otherwise dirt and body salts will clog up the pores. Try to use a very mild detergent or one of the specialist cleaning fluids – a strong detergent will act as a wicking agent and may lead to water entry. As long as a Gore-Tex garment is well-designed, is fairly lightweight yet durable, and is carried at all times when out on the hills, it should prove to be a very useful piece of outdoor kit for a mountain biker.

The same goes for Sympatex garments. This material breathes as well as Gore-Tex and in some cases can be made into more comfortable garments, thanks to Sympatex being a touch more flexible and a lot more stretchy. Whereas Gore-Tex is a 'perforated' fabric, Sympatex is a 'film' and is unperforated. It works by a hydrophilic action. Molecules of water vapour are attracted to the hydrophilic molecules in the

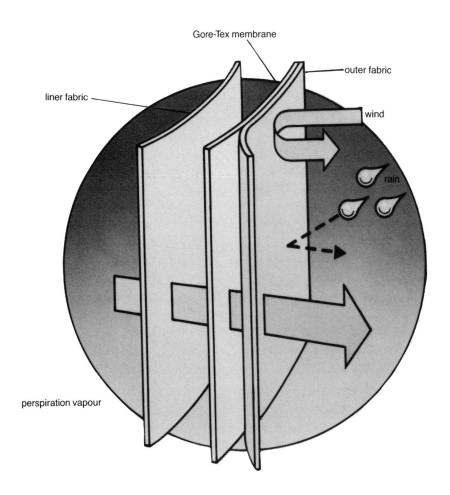

liner fabric

Gore-Tex membrane

outer fabric

wind

rain

perspiration vapour

Gore-Tex material.

film coating. This transports water vapour from the lower garments, at a great speed, through the shell via the molecular chains of the polyester copolymer film. This transportation of sweat is quick and efficient. The copolymer film is bonded, or laminated, to other fabrics and thanks to its inherent impermeability it enables an extremely high hydrostatic head to be achieved – in other words the material is waterproof. Of course anything that is waterproof is also, by definition, windproof (this equation does not work the other way round however!). So Sympatex, like Gore-Tex, can be made up into some very efficient shell garments. As it is not porous it cannot be clogged up with body oils or grime.

Climaguard clothing is effective and very lightweight.

Sympatex is the most expensive of the hydrophilic fabrics. The others are cheaper but then again they are nowhere near as effective. However, if price is a major consideration then breathable polyurethane coated fabrics from such companies as Peter Storm will be semi-breathable and relatively cheap. Peter Storm have sold over a million jackets in the UK – all of them made from breathable polyurethane materials. Whilst this does not attest to their effectiveness it does attest to their popularity. Basically they are cheap and cheerful and will be better than an unbreathable shell garment, but for mountain biking they cannot really cope with the large amounts of sweat generated.

Microfibre fabrics are a new generation of lightweight fabrics that, thanks to their woven manufacture, breathe very well indeed. There are many types available but the one I have had most experience with is Climaguard. The actual fibre is made from a very supple multifilament of polymide/nylon. The technology for its manufacture was developed in Switzerland by the textile company Rotofil. They spin the fibres into extremely fine yarns and then densely weave them, on new looms capable of 'packing' more yarns into a smaller space, into Climaguard. The resulting fabric therefore blocks wind well, is compactible and is breathable. Also, thanks to a surface treatment, it is also water-resistant. So long as rain is not too copious, water just forms into little mercury-like globules and rolls off the garment. This is because of surface tension – the molecules of water cannot penetrate the tightly-woven fabric or the proofing and so they regroup, form a globule and skid away. On fine windy days microfibre garments can act as good lightweight shells that will not 'sweat up'. Pertex is another material of this type and one which is widely available.

Thanks to companies such as Survival Aids the material Ventile – a compacted cotton fabric – is experiencing a renaissance at the moment. First developed during World War II as a material to protect ditched pilots, Ventile and other outdoor cotton fabrics went through a bad patch when polyurethane nylons and then Gore-Tex came on to the scene. Whilst Ventile is windproof, durable, flexible and breathable it has a tendency to waterlog if it gets too wet. When Ventile is rained upon a surface treatment sheds rain and the cotton fibres expand with the addition of water; the weave clamps up thereby preventing rain from entering. However, breathability is cut down when this happens and obviously the garment feels much heavier because of all the added water! Ventile, once thoroughly wet, will take an age to dry and is too bulky for taking on anything other than day tours – it is certainly not a garment for taking on extended bike expeditions. It is, however, practical for mountain biking because of its durability and tear-resistance. On windy days it could be a good shell garment for mucking around in – any falls from the bike onto rock or whatever may hurt you but the garment should come out pretty much unscathed!

All the fabrics mentioned above are better than polyurethane nylon or neoprene garments – mostly because they breathe. Mountain biking is too active a sport for non-breathable shell garments to even be considered for serious use. The wearer will feel clammy very quickly in a polyurethane nylon coat and this may cause the wearer to cool down excessively if he or she stops or rides downhill. Whilst such garments are cheap, buying them for mountain biking would be a false, and perhaps even dangerous, economy.

## Design Features to Look out for

Shell garments should be roomy so that the mid-layers can be worn comfortably. They should fit snugly down to just below the hips so that there is no flapping about further down the legs. Draw cords at the waist and at the bottom of the garment can make all the difference in converting a hill walking jacket into a mountain biking one. Cuffs should be windproof and should batten down well. I have found smock design shell garments to be the best for cycling in – the Sprayway ones are brilliant, as are the Berghaus Technique ones (Technique is a treated hydrophilic microfibre). Hoods are generally unusable for cycling in, but if downpours are severe they can be desirable. Make sure they can be positioned accurately and that they allow adequate head turns.

All garments should have their seams well sealed by taping. Just because a manufacturer uses one of the miracle materials does not mean the garment will be weatherproof – indeed, a couple of years ago W.L. Gore refused to supply one famous cycle jacket manufacturer with material, because the seams on the Gore-Tex garments it made were not sufficiently sealed. If a Gore-Tex garment is offered at a bargain price be especially careful and check it out well. Bear in mind that the manufacturer of good shell garments is labour intensive and is of a highly technical nature; prices, therefore, will tend to be high.

Shoulders on shell garments should be wide to accommodate the width of reach needed for handlebar positioning and the underarms should hang loose to further facilitate this breadth of movement. Check to make sure there are no seams on the shoulder points, otherwise leaks may occur. Ventilation is also important with shell clothing, so make sure there are zips on the bottom of the front opening as well as at the top – in other words a two-way zip. Air circulation from below can keep the wearer ventilated even when it is raining hard. It is important not to over-sweat so keep the garments well ventilated.

Beware of insulated Gore-Tex shell garments (or other types of waterproof fabric) – for instance ski jackets or smocks. Mountain bikers need mid-layers when it is cold rather than insulated garments. Many ski jackets do look good for mountain biking but a great deal are fashion-orientated and will perform badly in the hills. They will also tend to be too hot; and because the insulation comes with the shell it will be difficult to regulate the temperature.

Shell garments are important – choose the best you can afford.

Many shell fabrics come in different weights so go for the lighter ones. Heavier fabrics are more wear resistant but are too restricting and inflexible for active use. Crashes can be experienced in Gore-Tex garments that will bring tears to the eyes of the purchaser of a jacket worth £150 – falls and other such abrasions can tear and abrade shell fabrics. Sympatex is much tougher and more durable than Gore-Tex. However, on the whole synthetic shell garments are not rugged enough for repeated crashes – if you ride fast and hard and you crash often, then Ventile jackets may be the best compromise between protection against the weather and durability.

Shell garments are important, so choose the best that you can afford. Old and leaking shells can be resealed and reproofed if necessary.

**Note:** where clothing makes and materials have been named in this chapter it must be realised that circumstances and trade names change with an alarming regularity. For instance, at the time of writing, Capilene from the American firm, Patagonia can only be obtained by chance in certain shops. This is because the UK importers stopped bringing the stuff in. A new importer, Mountain Air, has recently been offering a limited selection of Patagonia clothes, including Capilene. The same is true for many other clothing types and materials. Where specific fabrics or brands have been mentioned this should only be taken as an example of what is available, and it may have to be a case of the individual doing a bit of personal research in the shops in his or her locality to find out what is available.

# 5 Short Tours

Entering and competing in organised mountain bike races can be physically rewarding and a lot of fun – but its thrill factor is pretty much short-lived. Touring, on the other hand, allows time for mellow reflection. Racing is a flash in the pan, over so quickly. Touring is an accumulation of fond memories, shared anecdotes, unhurried living. Racing is heads down and win. Touring is taking the time to savour views and meet people and experience places.

Touring 'off the beaten track' has been going on since the bicycle was first invented. Established organisations such as the Cyclist's Touring Club and the Rough Stuff Fellowship had been going off-road well before the designed-for-the-purpose mountain bike became fashionable. Eminent cycle tourists – such as the Hibells of this world – have enough off-road experience to keep us in anecdotes for years, but the bikes they managed their rambles upon were not really perfect for the job. They were 'beefed up' adaptations of touring bikes – custom built to take the knocks, but using adapted 'road' components. The true touring mountain bike on the other hand is off-road through and through – its laid-back geometry, wide, gripping tyres, heavy load-bearing capability and its sit-up-and-scan riding position make it purpose built for pure off-road cycling.

After my first mountain bike tour I was completely hooked and every tour since then has been undertaken on an ATB – even road tours. Yes, I know that sounds ridiculous – road touring on a mountain bike? I think however, that the ATB scores over the dropped handle-bar touring machine even on tarmac. For a start

the 'sit-up-and-scan' position is the natural touring pose. It has often been stated that as a cycle tourist gets older he or she graduates on to flat bars for comfort and an all-round viewing position. Well, mountain bikers have preceded the old age part and have gone straight for flat bars. This is firstly for leverage and control over rough ground and secondly for the wonderful views the straight back position gives.

The out-and-out racing bike will never die because it has a very specific usage. The touring bike, on the other hand, has no such safety from extinction. In style and design it is little more than an adapted racer, whilst the true ATB is as far removed from a racer as a diamond framed bicycle can be. It is my prediction that within about ten years there will be more ATBs used for tarmac touring than standard machines – anyone who has been to America recently will back me up on that. Also, of course, when off-road conditions are encountered the ATB touring bike is already designed to be capable of the roughest rough stuff.

Expeditioning on mountain bikes has to be the best of ATB experiences – but not everyone can hop on their bike and spend six months away in some exotic spot. Most people have to make do with day or weekend tours in this country. Yet given the amazing variety of the British Isles, travel here is no poor cousin to travelling in foreign parts. On trips abroad I travel a lot by myself – then it is only myself I have to worry about – but one of the greatest things about day tours in this country is that they can be so sociable. Usually myself and a group of friends agree to meet on a Sunday

Mountain bike touring – a day tour in the Lake District.

Even on day tours you should carry a bit more than this.

morning and if we are not planning to go too far then we will leave the deciding of destinations until the last minute. Four or five hour sorties across the local hills and moors can be intensely satisfying. For more distant trips – for instance a trip to the Lake District, a couple of hours away by car – we plan a couple of days ahead and then just pray for good weather.

One day last summer a group of us agreed to spend a day in the Lakes. It was the first hot day of summer – just about a week after British Summer Time had crept in unannounced (most days were still in the depths of winter). We had taken two cars and had set out early in the morning in the general direction of Cumbria. The previous day had been nice and sunny, but none of us were under any illusions as to getting the same sort of weather two days in a row. It

was bound to pour down the minute we arrived within sight of a decent off-road route. That was the way it normally happened, so why think any differently? But on this day we unloaded the bikes and it was sunny. This felt strange. We cycled off, wearing little else but sunglasses and skin tights. It was also still sunny – very strange.

The sunshine continued and it stayed with us all day. We even came home pink and lobster looking – the first sunburn of the year! Our route involved getting up on to High Street (coming up from Pooley Bridge). This bridle-way is normally swamped with walkers and this is one of the reasons we very rarely bother to come to the Lakes on a weekend. But on this occasion luck was on our side, for despite a glorious day, a favourable weather forecast and firm ground underfoot, we were virtually alone

Day tours can be suited to the spirit of every rider, so they are always enjoyable.

up on the hilltops. We saw some horse riders, a few groups of ramblers and the odd individual walker but, apart from that, nobody else. In the Lakes this would be unusual on a winter weekday in the pouring rain – on a sunny semi-summer's day it was no less than miraculous!

We took full advantage of our fortune and let our fat tyres roll fast over some stunning descents, and some not quite so stunning ascents. Mick as the group photographer, could not resist firing off shot after shot and so, despite the odd few interludes of kamikaze descending, we had a fairly relaxing day of stopping when the fancy took us and generally lazing about in the sun – hence the red noses and sunburned features in the photos. However, on one of the more hair-raising descents we were anything but lazy – for a start I was coming down faster than I would normally think sane. Grinning and then

groaning in rapid succession I would skim round one bend, bump the bike off a rock or two, and then continue down at breakneck speed on the firm gravel track. About two miles from the bottom of the particular valley we were riding through and cycling too fast to stop quickly, I sped down into a hollow and then spotted an obstacle looming ahead. I tried to bunny-hop over the obstacle – a stretch of stagnant, black mud – I failed miserably.

My front wheel went in down to its axle and I departed from the saddle at a huge rate of knots. At what seemed an opportune split second I spread my legs wide and Cossack-jumped clear of the handlebars, landing on my shoulder and rolling into the soft bank none the worse for wear. To retrieve my free-standing bike I squelched down into the mud and pulled the machine free. It came out with a resounding 'plop'. To my surprise the mud was exceedingly warm and even felt quite pleasant – although it was not until later that we collectively found out that it had a subtle, yet completely overpowering, after-smell that seemed to worsen as the afternoon wore on. Two solitary walkers, who were sitting quietly at the side of a little stream that trickled gently down the valley fifty feet to our right, looked at us with bemusement. They had the sort of look on their faces that suggested they had seen it all before.

We continued downhill, with Dave leading now, and roller-coastered along a hard-packed track that occasionally had us jumping a good few feet through the air, as hidden rocks suddenly leaped out at us. The descent was fast and furious, which was welcome because most of the previous few hours had been patient, methodical ascending. Our rims became red-hot as we braked and sped, braked and sped, along the track. At one point our downhill route petered out into a grassy bank that was too steep to cycle down without ripping up the turf by skidding. This was the only part of the day we had to walk but it was soon over. The rest of

Mountain bikes can be transported on a car roof-rack.

the descent was on grass but it was an extremely tough and dry type of grass and showed not a mark of our passing, even when back brakes had to be locked up. The views coming down the valley were incredibly beautiful and, of course, were immortalised on film by our official team photographer.

By four o'clock we were down off the 'mountains' and, sadly, back on tarmac. Down the road a bit we came to a low, five-tiered stone bridge, under which flowed an enticing stream of cool, clear, fast moving water. It looked a perfect spot for rinsing the bikes down – and, as it turned out, rinsing each other down as well! After the frolicking was over we climbed from the water, shook the bikes dry and then pedalled along to the Ullswater Yacht Club where we met up with windsurfer extra-

ordinaire Lester Noble (of Orange bikes fame), who had completed the same route as us only an hour previously. He kindly offered to teach me how to windsurf. I politely declined – I mentioned the fact that I would rather just stick to fat tyres.

# WEEKENDS AWAY

Short tours – of say two or three days (aren't Bank Holiday weekends wonderful) – can also be an enormous amount of fun. The equipment needed for them is little different to that needed for a day tour. That is, unless you are camping out in which case you may need plenty of luggage space to carry tents and the like. One of my fondest memories of weekend touring is of the

A rucksack full of gear is all that is needed for a short tour.

couple of days Mick Craig and I spent skimming around the North York Moors. We decided not to carry camping gear and instead used bed and breakfast accommodation. The following is a description of that weekend and for me it sums up the many pleasures to be had on short tours.

The weather had turned out to be truly beautiful so I had felt compelled to insert my brand new contact lenses. I was supposed to 'wear them in' for a bit first – which in effect meant I had to restrict the amount of time they were put in for each day, but this two-day bike tour was just too visually stunning for me to stick, at all strictly, to the lens wear guide-lines. The young women sitting on beach towels twenty feet away, seemed to be laughing at us – and who can blame them, after all cyclists wearing little black shorts and riding day-glo bicycles are not

exactly the most conservative of sights. As Mick had just been observed helping me put my contact lenses in and not wanting to be the cause of any more unintentional jocularity, we decided discretion was the better part of valour and mounted our embarrassingly colourful bikes and pedalled off up the steep, sand-peppered, tarmacadamed road.

We were in picturesque Staithes on the North Yorkshire coast and were not too sure of the off-road route out of the town. Unfortunately in our endeavours to leave, we had to make four or five swoops past the by now hysterical young females. Luckily we had our 'blackout' shades on, so our red faces would have been quite well disguised – mind you I think my legs were blushing. Mick, bless his little cotton socks (Castelli ones of course!), found the exit out and so off we sped, glad to be on the go again. This exit was a narrow, dirt path that snaked its way up the sea cliff. Our 2.125s tractored us to the top and then the ups-and-downs began once more. All along our chosen route that day we had been swooping and diving along a fourteen inch track that lay sandwiched between fenced-off farmland on one side and sea cliffs on the other. Concentration was vital – on some sections a slip would have meant a fall to the sea a few hundred feet below. On most of the track, though, there was a reassuring strip of grass that shielded us from the edge. We felt safe enough to abandon caution to the wind and the undulating cliffs provided a ride that can only be compared to being on an erratic roller-coaster. We both still agree that these few hours of ups and downs were the finest we have ever come across.

They also led to one of the funniest crashes we have had – and we certainly have not had a shortage of those! Mick, who was leading a fast drop down into a hollow, suddenly decided, in his wisdom, to jam his brakes on. As I was about two seconds behind him I did not think it was all that wise, but before any avoiding action could

The author repairing a North York Moors induced puncture.

be taken, and realising anyway that there was nowhere to go but forward, the 'cause and effect' rule came into play. The 'cause' was Mick coming to a very sudden halt, which he later blamed on a tree root, and the 'effect' was me flying through the air devoid of bicycle. I grazed my forehead, bruised my pride and dented my bike but other than that I was fine. Why people laugh after incidents such as these I will never really fathom – but laugh we did, uncontrollably. Maybe it is the relief of surviving unscathed?

We had started that morning from Saltburn – a short train journey away from our home town of Newcastle. Right from the start of the first climb we knew this weekend was going to be a good one. It felt wonderful to be away from work, stress and all the other pains of twentieth century living – with food, tools and the odd bit of spare clothing in our rucksacks we felt totally free and the weekend lived up to all our expectations. Touring by bike is something I have long enjoyed – it gives an all-over sense of freedom like few others. Touring abroad is obviously exciting but for sheer relaxation day and weekend tours in this country are hard to beat; it is amazing the amount of things you can pack into a long weekend.

On this particular weekend we rode hell for leather on the first day, not for any desire for speed or competition, but just because the terrain suggested it. Up hill and down dale, as it were, will never be relaxing because so much effort is involved. We rode hard and fast till mid-afternoon when we at last reached Whitby. Then after an ice-cream or two we took the train from Whitby station to Grosmont in the North York Moors. At a much more leisurely pace we followed the railway path that disappears out of Grosmont for a few miles until we reached our destination for the day – Goathland. Here we knew there was plenty of accommodation and to top it all off a genuine, idyllic waterfall. On reaching the sheep-strewn village green we sat ourselves down, completed a few bike repairs, ate ourselves silly in a café and then booked into a pleasant and homely bed & breakfast.

With the last few dregs of energy we had left we managed to make it down to the waterfall that gurgled away not far from the village green. The way down to the falls was via numerous elongated steps, made from hard-packed dirt and bolstered up by planks of wood. We cycled ('bounced' would be closer to the mark) just about all the way to the falls in a fraction of the time it would have taken to walk. The waterfall was extremely photogenic and naturally demanded a few poses for posterity. Getting back up the steps was more strenuous, but possible nevertheless, and within twenty minutes we were back in our cosy little B&B. After showering we hobbled out to the local hostelry and partook of the area's finest ales. As Mick only had a pair of woollen tights to act as trousers we did not really wonder why we were again the centre of attention. I do not suppose my lurid, fluorescent pink Been Bag top helped much either!

The next morning we set off nice and early. With a full English breakfast inside us we powered our way across the desolate moors and save for a few thousand sheep we were all but alone. This part of the North York Moors is strewn with wheel-buckling rocks and we had great fun bunny-hopping our way across all these obstacles. I put my foot down a few times. Mick never. Within four or five hours of such riding we were back on tarmac again and by chance, not design, we found ourselves spinning effortlessly downhill, for a number of miles, to our destination railway station. Exhausted, we climbed aboard the first train that chuntered in. A couple of hours later we were back in sunny Newcastle.

Whilst it is fun to ride with other people it can also be good to ride solo. In my case I often do not have much choice. Being a freelance journalist, who works odd hours, no potential biking

Solo riding can be good.

partners are free when I am free. So, in mid-week office hours I pedal on the hills when everybody else is at work. This is good if you do not want to meet anyone else on the hills, but it does mean that cycling partners cannot join you in your ride. Solo can be nice though. On my solitary rides I normally go over to the moors above Blanchland. Some days I will enjoy myself immensely; on others I wish for company. On one winter's day last year I went out on to the moors solo and discovered a thing or two about myself.

One moment I was joyfully pedalling along in the middle of nowhere trying my level best to keep a jolting mountain bike out of the unfathomable depths of the numerous mud pools arrayed before me, and the next I had somer-saulted over the handlebars and executed a near-perfect head plant into a clump of slimy heather. Heavy rain was belting down on all sides and my front wheel was now more than a little skew-whiff – I had buckled it by running over a hidden bump, at speed, just to the side of a moorland track. Visibility was almost nil because of a large amount of menacingly low cloud and of course the rain that results from such cloud; the ambient air temperature, as they say, was none too warm. Civilisation, or at least somewhere that had a wheel-trueing jig, was many miles away and despite all my wet weather gear I was soaked through. Even so, I had to fix the bike – not an appealing prospect given the general inclemency. However, I am not a natural mechanic – only when it really is the very last option will I attempt my own repairs. This, unfortunately, was such an occasion and despite the locale and the weather being as far removed from a nice, cosy workshop as I could have imagined I had to spread out my tools and get to work on trueing the wheel.

Providentially, as soon as I had started on my impromptu bike surgery, the rain halted in its persistent attempts to drown me and the sun, previously unseen all day, bounced out from behind the clouds and made everything around me sparkle and gleam. A tiny watery rainbow appeared off in the distance and did its best to gladden my day. All the surrounding scenery became animated and the beautiful colours of the hills and moors became surprisingly intense. Even the numerous muddy puddles gave off the odd glint of reflected sunshine. As if inspired I chanced upon the correct permuta-tion of spoke tightening and spoke loosening and within twenty minutes of the crash I was fat-tyre pedalling again. The weather held out for a further few minutes although the incle-mency soon returned to keep me company.

Even though I live and work in that sup-posedly blighted black spot, Newcastle, I am within easy reach of some of the most unspoilt and most unpopulated stretches of countryside in England – the hill areas of Northumberland. I could now quote to you from some guidebook or other about the acreage of land this area encom-passes, or the flora and fauna to be found or even the soil types encountered, but I will not bother. Suffice to say that it is wild hill country with all the beauties, and problems, that that entails.

I had come across from Newcastle via the very pretty Derwent river valley and now I was a few miles away from the small village of Blanchland. I usually avoid this sort of off-road riding if it is really pouring down because of the lack of adequate braking power and the chance I may come into contact with something, or somebody, harder than heather. A mountain bike is also more likely to damage the exposed earth when there has been a lot of rain. On this occasion however, I had started out in fairish weather and the previous night's forecast by the weathermen had not predicted this amount of rainfall in any of its details.

After coming down off the hills, happy at dis-covering a hitherto unknown talent for bike fixing in adversity and at the same time witnes-

The solo rider.

sing a glorious interlude of scenic splendours, albeit too brief, I had a well-earned paddle in the river at Blanchland and gave the bruised and battered bike a nice wash. With all the rain still pouring forth I lifted the bike from the river, propped it up in the middle of the village, bought some energy-restoring fruit, and then sat perched on a wall with an immense smile on my face – it had been a good day. Ten or so saddled up horses and their hard-hatted and bedraggled riders plodded past and looked at me with frowns on their sad and wet faces – they could not work out from the state of me why I was quite so happy. The bike was hidden from view behind the wall and I was perched on the edge, eating a banana, with my little legs dangling – to them the perfect village idiot. I vocalised my greetings, got nothing in return and they continued to file past me totally unaware that they were looking at the happiest day-touring mountain biker in the world.

# 6 Essential Touring Equipment for Mountain Bikers

(Equip for Adventure)

Adventure will sometimes come to you; but more often than not you will have to go to it. Moping around the house day-dreaming about exotic locations will get you nowhere. The thrill of travelling will only come about when you are actually out there living it. The following may sound obvious but it is surprising how many people just think about using their mountain bikes as an expedition machine. The thinkers stay at home and watch the television; the doers get a sun-tan. They also gain a lifetime of experience.

Doing something about the irresistible urge to travel involves will-power and determination. It is no less than a positive frame of mind. If you are determined enough you can achieve anything – maybe you will be the first mountain biker to haul his or her machine to the top of Everest? Or maybe not, but dreaming will only get you there if it acts as a mind-drama, subliminally persuading you to take the first step.

Equipment choice is secondary to the initial spark of originality but it can be an important choice. Load up with the wrong gear and you may very well get no further than the airport departure lounge. Choosing which items to pack and which to discard is an immensely personal thing. However, even for the shortest of weekend tours there are a few basic items which should be regarded as vital. The check-list below gives them in order of priority.

## 'Ultra, Ultra-lightweight' Touring Check-list

**Off-road mountain bike**   Make, model and colours immaterial, but padded saddles and cushioned handlebar grips are essential.

**Set of clothing**   This can be bike wear only if travelling in hot climes, although do carry long trousers if you venture into Muslim domains.

**Valid passport**   Try and get as many visas as possible (if needed) in this country rather than having to queue abroad. If you need visas in a hurry contact one of the visa shops listed in the Useful Addresses section.

**Note:** all other items of equipment, including money, tools, spares, tents, sleeping bags etc. are completely optional.

Tours, of any duration above two or three days, undertaken solely with the items above will be exciting – mostly because of the wholly lackadaisical attitude to the non-carrying of touring paraphernalia. Exciting and perhaps even carefree, but if choosing this option then it would be advisable to at least include a sizeable wad of fivers. In this country, and in most places where 'civilisation' (shops, pubs, hotels, garages etc.) exists, money can buy you out of most situations. In more extreme and remote circumstances, however, no amount of money can

A rucksack can be good for lightweight expeditions.

Make sure your expedition bike is strong enough to take a lot of punishment.

A Blackburn rack can hold anything!

guarantee survival. So, there is a natural progression from the 'ultra, ultra-lightweight' method of bike packing to the 'ultra-lightweight' version. The check-list for this second method, the first on the scale of sensibility, is somewhat more provisioned.

# 'Ultra-lightweight' Touring Check-list

**Basics** *See* 'Ultra, Ultra-lightweight' Touring Check-list.
**Money** As much as you can spare and do not forget the plastic.
**Panniers or rucksack** Total capacity approximately twenty to forty litres.

**Long trousers** Lightweight, windproof and packable, for example Rohan Bags. Women may also find trousers more suitable.
**Windproof and/or warm top** Depending on weather conditions expected, lightweight and versatile, for example Rohan Moving On, Mountain Equipment Ultrafleece or Calange Polarlite.
**Lightweight waterproof top** May be breathable nylon such as one of the microfibre jackets, for example Karrimor Climaguard.
**Water purifying tablets** Iodine ones are best but do not overdose on them or take them for long periods as you will get iodine poisoning, which is possibly worse for your long-term health than the parasites in the water!

**Small amount of energy food** Semi-dried stick bananas are my favourite.

**Mini wash kit** For instance Body Wash soap and a Body Shop mini-toothbrush. No need for a towel, use your clothes instead!

**Maps and compass** Useful in most places, except perhaps if you are planning a trip to the Cuillin Ridge in Skye (iron deposits make the compass needle go haywire).

**Essential tools** This should be a judicious selection. Heavy items are discarded or replaced by a do-it-all tool such as the Leatherman (available from Survival Aids).

**Hat, sunglasses, sun-tan lotion, insect repellent and other medications** If needed.

This sort of equipment list is adequate for touring virtually anywhere in the world and for any length of time. It is adequate for most eventualities, but cannot guarantee comfort if hotels or guesthouses are not found or if shops cannot be reached. The limited amount of clothing will also mean frequent laundry days (use biodegradable products such as Survival Aids' 'Body Wash' or Cosmetics-To-Go 'Africa Wash'). Extended downpours or freak weather conditions are not catered for either. But this type of equipment list makes a useful lightweight kit that is adequate enough for short weekend tours where civilisation is not too far away from the off-road route. For more extended tours such packing would lead to a degree of discom-

Lightweight travelling.

fort because of the lack of 'luxury' items such as sleeping bags. When staying in out-of-the-way inns, hotels or villagers' huts a sleeping bag is an effective and polite way of avoiding bed bugs, lice and fleas.

The average bike traveller is the one who carries equipment at one level above the 'ultra-lightweight' method. This third category is the one to which I belong; I am a lightweight bike traveller. For weekend tours I will be ultra-lightweight but for any tour lasting more than two days or so (and especially if I am abroad) I would be loathe not to pack a few items considered 'luxurious' by the very hardy biker. There is not enough space to list every last knick-knack I take but the following are the most important items – most important to me, that is.

# 'Lightweight' Touring Check-list

**(Include most items from the previous check-lists)**

**Sleeping bag**   A lightweight bag, such as the Rab goosedown, offers no bulky extras such as zips, and weighs next to nothing. It packs down to the size of a small loaf.

**Bivvysac**   Gore-Tex ones are best and are great for sleeping out under the stars. But if you do not like bugs use a lightweight tent instead. If travelling with company the weight of a three person tent becomes very low when shared out.

**Stove, fuel, lightweight pots and pans** Personally I never carry any cooking equipment whatsoever. If it is cold and wet outside, a warm drink is psychologically satisfying but its warming effect is negligible. Indeed the calorific burn of cold drinks and food is just the same as hot ones. So, instead of barbecuing and boiling, I normally picnic! When touring in Zambia, Gil, my companion, could build wonderful camp-fires (even out of damp wood) so we had roaring fires every night. If nothing else it kept the

animals away and it was wonderful to fall asleep beside the dying embers. We were also able to toast bread the next morning by shoving a slice or two down into the ashes!

**Tool-kit and spares**   Allen keys, lightweight spanners, pliers (the aforementioned Leather-man tool has pliers and a number of other tools attached), chain breaking tool, screwdriver, spoke key. Most jobs can be tackled with these tools. Such items as freewheel removers or cone spanners are too heavy to lug around – cones can be adjusted by an adjustable spanner and if your freewheel needs removing you are in trouble anyway. There are many jobs that even a fully provisioned bike tourist would find difficult, so it is hard to insure against every eventuality by the carrying of extra tools and extraction implements. If you are stuck in the middle of nowhere, you may have to bodge a repair to get you to the next outpost of civilisa-tion. Once there however, it is comforting to note that there are not many places in the world that will be without a workshop in the vicinity.

**Heavyweight waterproof**   Maybe Gore-Tex or Sympatex. The latter reacts better than Gore-Tex to being creased after being stuffed in a pannier time after time.

**Water bags**   For hot climes only; the Liquipak ones are by far the best.

Taking more equipment than this will make the bike difficult to control. Less adventurous routes will have to be taken because the bumping and jolting of a good off-road track will soon punish a bike that is overloaded. Pedalling such an obese bike is not fun; overload at your peril. Even when adventure touring with just a couple of small pannier bags you should not attempt any trick riding – these antics are fun when at home and within limping distance of your local bike shop but they are not advisable when you are out in the sticks. Discounting the fact that such trick riding would be tough when loaded up anyway, it must be noted that neither

Pannier bags are better than rucksacks for longer tours.

Shimano Deore XT 2 brakes – powerful enough to halt a heavily-laden mountain biker.

Equip your machine with the strongest and best componentary available – Shimano gears are very practical.

you nor your machine are in any way likely to be put back together again if anything untoward happens. You have got to travel very much within the capabilities of the loaded-up machine.

Taking such spares as rear derailleurs, spindles, hubs, tyres and the like would obviously give peace of mind but it would be far simpler to equip your machine with the strongest and best componentary available. Other items you may find useful are included in the final check-list. These can be used along with the basic check-lists above to create a 'mix-and-match' touring selection. Some of these items can be regarded as potentially superfluous – I certainly would not take all of them. Items such as short-wave radios (see the Survival Aids catalogue) or even Walkmans could be useful if you get bored easily but their usefulness would very much seem to be in the eye of the beholder (sic). I would never even consider taking them.

# Miscellaneous Check-list

**First-aid kit**   The Gregson Pack is the best first-aid kit on the market. It is bulky but could be worth it.

**Syringe kit**   If you intend to travel in the Third World, carrying a syringe kit, such as the MASTA one, is sensible. The risk of AIDS is a real one in places such as Africa. Unsterilised needles may be used on you if you have an accident and need surgery or injections, or if you have to visit a dentist. Sterile sutures are also included in the MASTA pack.

**Camera and accessories**   Heavy and cumbersome and a nuisance in wet or sandy areas. The compact cameras are lighter and easier to use but do not offer the same versatility as a good 35mm SLR. If you want to get your trip shots published take transparency films and protect them from sunlight, water, heat and Third World X-ray machines (the ones in developed countries are normally safe for films up to a rating of 1000 ASA). An all-in-one zoom and wide-angle lens (28–70mm) is a good all-rounder but consider taking a real wide-angle as well for the beautiful landscapes you will be travelling through. In sunny countries take a polarising filter and swivel it to get the really blue-black skies.

**Earplugs**   For long-haul flights, noisy hotel rooms or when the sounds of nature outside your tent start to annoy you, these can be a godsend.

**Stationery**   In twenty years' time you may want to refresh your memory of how adventurous you were. Photos are OK, but there is nothing like a vividly written journal. So take an exercise book and jot down all your thoughts. And do not forget paper and pen to note down the addresses of people you meet on the way.

Anything else? Of course there is but that is for you to decide. Bike-packing is a personal affair and feel free to ignore any advice that people, including myself, give you. To find your own comfort level you would have to experiment with a few weekend tours to see what you can easily live without. Do bear in mind though that all the stuff you lay out on your bedroom floor ready for your first adventure – and all of which looks pretty vital to you – can make your bike handle like a pig. Pack everything you think you will need into your panniers, test the laden bike out and if you are not happy with the resulting ride, empty the panniers and clinically assess the worth of every single item. If in doubt, chuck it out! On my first ever tour abroad I left a trail of abandoned gear right the way through Europe! Since then I have rationalised my gear down to the barest minimum. In photographs my bike may look fully loaded but in actual fact the panniers are only half full of UK-shipped

A custom built touring stem.

The off-road 'bouncy' stem can alleviate wrist problems on a touring mountain bike.

which had been lacerated by the sharp volcanic rock. As a spare, a foldable knobbly with a Kevlar bead is ideal – it is expensive but it packs down well. One alternative to carrying a spare is to post one ahead to a centrally-located major post office – via poste restante. For circular tours this arrangement is fine; for one-way crossings it can be a hassle if you have a blow-out thousands of miles from the post office.

Racks for expedition use need to be the strongest available. Alloy carriers, such as the Blackburn, are incredibly strong but if they should happen to break they are next to impossible to repair adequately. A much cheaper alternative is to use a couple of bog-standard, steel-carriers, such as those made by Karrimor. They are heavier than aluminium racks but their main advantage lies in the fact that they can be welded back together again after a breakage. Steel carriers could also be strengthened before departure by the addition of struts and so forth and your local bike builder or metal workshop will do this for you quite cheaply. Extra strength is nice, but then again, if the amount you are loading into your panniers is likely to break a sturdy rack, you are carrying too much anyway!

So, you have decided on all your equipment for your tour. Have you overloaded? Trying to get a bike through an airport check-in without it getting weighed is one way to avoid excess baggage payments. Another way is to travel ultra-lightweight. Flying with a bike is not as bad as is often made out. I have had very few real problems. There is a catch however – bikes and bike luggage often weigh more than 22kg (the limit for an individual). If you are asked to pay excess plead poverty or cause a distraction, do anything – if you do not, it will cost you an arm, a leg and half the holiday money!

Coming back from Morocco two years ago I was charged an amazing amount of excess – I said I could not and would not pay. Because of my bleatings they let me repack my in-flight bag

stuff; the other half will be filled with locally-bought food and many bags of water. After your first real tour this sort of rationalisation becomes easy. You do not realise that much of your potential gear is superfluous until you have lugged it around for a few days, so do some trial runs before embarking on any major sorties into the great wide yonder. Either that or take a sag wagon (support vehicle).

To make the ride more bearable a good expedition mountain bike should have the thickest tyres possible fitted, both for comfort and for traction. And if you are heading off to lands where tyres regularly get shredded then at least one spare is a necessary precaution. In Iceland a couple of years ago I saw an over-abundance of abandoned cycle and vehicle tyres

You can have your bar bag holder welded to your handlebars.

so I went through Casablanca customs with just about all of my luggage strapped to my body. I was extremely over the limit because I had bought some Bedouin carpets as presents, yet because I had complained I was allowed through looking like a cross between the Michelin man and a pregnant Geoff Capes! Likewise at the Aeroflot check-in desk in Lusaka, Zambia, an Israeli companion and myself persuaded the Russian clerk to let us through without having to pay excess – although it was such a struggle that we were the last ones to be allowed to book in and by that time the customs officials had closed down for the day. It was a pretty frantic affair rushing around Lusaka airport searching for any rubber-stamping officials with the power to grant us the numerous exit visas and currency control slips that would enable us to fly

out. So, sometimes not paying excess can be a bit of a headache – but, as cycle tourists are usually on a very restricted budget, making the extra fuss is always worth it.

Just in case the bike does get weighed (sometimes Heathrow staff do so, as will the Swiss) take as much off it as possible and carry it as hand luggage. I always put the heaviest touring equipment in my in-flight bag – for instance the tools and so forth – although it can be quite embarrassing if it arouses suspicions when it goes through the X-ray machine and you have to empty out a bag that has been packed full, just to get down into the tool-kit. The staff at Cairo airport did not bat an eyelid when the tool-kit showed up on one of their little screens but Geneva was not so laid back. If you are travelling in a group then all the luggage of the group can be taken together (if the airport staff insist on weighing it that is) and the rounded-up total should never exceed the limit.

Bike objects can definitely look odd in an airport situation – I do not just mean Lycra skin shorts! For instance, hide your 'frame-fit' pump out of sight. I once received a few startled stares and the quick attention of some security guards when I wandered through Schipol airport in Amsterdam with a high-pressure pump that they thought doubled as a machine gun – a lot of the passengers-to-be were also prone to giving me a wide berth!

The subject of packing your bike away into a cardboard box is a problematical one. Most of the time it is not necessary and is hardly ever enforced. The only airline I have travelled with who specify that you completely strip down your bike and pack it in a cardboard box job is Swissair. The rest have opinions that are either non-committal and they can be persuaded, given time and tact, to take the bike whole – or the staff could not care less and let you do as you wish. Before handing your bike over to the luggage handler, twist the handlebars round so they are in line with the top tube, deflate the tyres to about ten pounds per square inch (the holds of aircraft are sometimes unpressurised) and take one pedal off. This last tactic is to prevent over-enthusiastic luggage handlers pedalling on your machine – something that is common in countries outside of Europe. Some bike tourists do advocate the strip-down job but I find that keeping the bike whole is far safer.

Elliptical chainrings can improve the ride for a tourer.

The handlers can see it is a bike and will not throw it around as much as they would throw around an incognito cardboard, or wooden box. And in order to protect other peoples' luggage, a bike (without a box) is usually put on top of the hold and more often than not comes out of the aircraft first. It is great to put some air into the fat tyres, hook the panniers back on, spanner about a bit and then shoot off out of the airport before other people have even received their luggage!

For long flights take on board your water bottle so that you can ask the hostesses to fill it with a fresh supply of water. Dehydration is one cause of airsickness and jetlag. On Aeroflot's African service the hostesses bring round some fizzy drinks in a jug that can be requested throughout the flight – but they take cups away all the time so a water bottle comes in handy. I now also take on board my water bags – when filled with air they make great travel pillows. One last tip on air travel – if you prefer real food, always order a vegetarian meal when you go travelling (book via the airline twenty-four hours in advance). For some reason a vegetarian meal on an aircraft is usually made fresh and is totally different to the food normally served up.

Flying with a bike and luggage need not be as difficult as would be imagined. On regular commercial flights it will be, so to speak, plain sailing. It is only on chartered flights (when travelling cheaply on the same flights as 'package tourists') that real problems arise – here the full bike strip-down and strict weighing-in are usually enforced. Try, wherever possible, to avoid such flights. So, on the whole, exotic lands are within easy reach for the mountain biker willing to transport his or her machine via the airlines of the world. For the most part it is not cheap but the adventure at the end of it will be more than worth it.

This chapter is not really meant to inform you exactly how to expedition or tell you exactly what to take – there are plenty of books that will explain all that (*see* Further Reading). It is just a basic introduction to the subject and only trial and error will tell you the rest. Equipment choice is important, but it is not everything. The get-up-and-go impulse is by far the most important characteristic of a bike traveller. Whereas some people buy all the best gear and then never use it in anger, the bona fide bike traveller will go on out there and enjoy himself, or herself, with or without adequate equipment.

I firmly believe that going on a mountain bike expedition – solo or in a small group – is one of the best ways to spend a week, a month, a year or a lifetime and it is open to anybody with the initiative. There are plenty of bikes to choose from, thousands of items of camping gear to access and innumerable destinations to be evaluated, and with a little foresight, a modicum of planning and the right state of mind you too can go have yourself an adventure. You will send me a postcard won't you?

# 7 Expeditions Awheel

Mountain bike expeditioning – I like that expression; it conjures up a mental picture of the khaki-clad bike explorer, sand-blown eyes narrowed against the glare and small beads of sweat mingling with grit on his or her sun-scorched brow.

The most heavily publicised bicycle expeditionists – the Crane cousins – are definitely straight out of a *Boy's Own Annual*. They are the perfect embodiment of the romantic ideal. Their background, with a patriarch persuading them into all sorts of scrapes from a very early age, is certainly the stuff heroes are made of (English ones anyway!). Their amazing escapades may seem foolhardy to armchair critics, but to most people they are an inspiration. Their get-up-and-go outlook on life, and reassuring ability to overcome any challenge with gusto, and the good old-fashioned British stiff upper lip is widely admired, and rightly so.

The Cranes may be the most famous two-wheeled explorers but there are scores of similar, although less well-publicised, cyclists out there, pedalling mountain bikes to the craziest, and most exciting, of places; which does not mean just Africa, South America or Asia – just as much adventure can be had far closer to home. Iceland say, or the remoter parts of Europe (including Scotland or France) all offer the intrepid ATBer plenty to feel adventurous about. Of course they are slightly chillier – in hot countries you can afford to carry a lot less luggage!

Now, you have bought this book because you are an avid mountain biker or are thinking of becoming one, so I will not relate to you in great detail the many merits a mountain bike has to offer over the traditional rough-stuff touring machine for expeditions and the like. Suffice to say that the trusty mountain bike can transport you and your luggage over the most hostile of terrain in more comfort, in more safety and in more style than the meatiest touring bikes. However, it must not be forgotten that cycle travel pioneers, such as the redoubtable Ian Hibell, have been circumnavigating the wilder parts of this globe for years on decrepit touring bikes. It worked for them. But, although I am not sure they would agree, I firmly believe a mountain bike would have made such trips so much easier and possibly even more enjoyable. So, let us take it as read that you are convinced of the benefits of mountain bikes for most long-haul, off-road expeditions, what next? Well, I guess the question will be, which bike – out of the multitude that are available – will be the best for you to explore upon?

Let us get this straight, you do not need an ultra-light, made-to-measure, specially strengthened and designed for the job ATB – but, for touring it can help! I stress touring because for most other ATBing occasions a £400 bike is adequate. It is quite straightforward – if you have the money (which means from £700 to over £1000) go for a custom-built bike; they are reliable, supremely strong and can have as many touring fittings as you like. For example low-rider carrier bosses, four or five sets of water bottle cage bosses, strategically placed pump-pegs and so on.

If you cannot get your hands on this sort of cash then going out into the great wide yonder on a standard machine is no big problem, and so long as all the moving parts are in good working order and the frame is not about to drop apart, will be just as enjoyable – if not more so, con-

The West Highland Way – an expedition north of the border.

Rob Orr is a true mountain bike expeditionist, having toured Europe and Israel.

sidering you have saved all that money! Doing up a standard, off-the-peg ATB for a trans-Sahara crossing, a mountain bike perusal of Peru or a serious sortie to the Scottish Highlands is still going to be costly though – racks will have to be bought, the transmission may have to be replaced (if worn down or mangled), water bottle cages will have to be fitted and a bike builder may have to add some extra braze-ons to a frame not wholly kitted out for touring. Then, of course, you could set out on a total wreck, if that is how you like to travel!

The very hardy, natural traveller could set off tomorrow at the drop of a hat, with one set of clothing, a decrepit bike and without any cash and yet still have a great time – with not a care in the world. If the bike falls apart, a repair is bodged and if cash runs out, so what? The truly

intrepid do not need cash – they will just beg, borrow or do a few odd jobs. I have journeyed with cycle travellers like this and they are the most incredible people you could ever meet. A few years ago I cycled for a week through the beautiful Kibbutz-strewn hinterland of Israel with a Californian hippy who had started out from the States with the best equipment Californian money could buy. By the time he had cycled half-way across Europe he had given it all away, including his hand-built mountain bike, and was cycling on an ancient single speed Swiss roadster that had obviously seen better days. Pinned to the flimsy rear rack was a minuscule rucksack which contained all his worldly possessions: a passport, a nylon cagoule, a circle of pitta bread, a few green olives and a threadbare woollen jumper – and

Heavy duty touring luggage.

Mountain bikes can go anywhere.

that was it! He had no long trousers to his name and the cotton shirt he wore was a cast-off from the second-hand bin of a Dutch commune. When he became hungry, passers-by (or even café owners!) would invariably offer him free food. When he really became desperate he would work for a few days here and there, on one of the many fruit-picking farms dotted around Europe. He had been living like this for nearly a year before I met him on Mount Carmel, near Haifa, and he would not have swapped his way of life for all the tea-bags in Streatham! The best bikes, the 'snazziest', most up-to-date equipment and a wad of traveller's cheques stuffed down the seat tube in case of emergencies, would have meant little to him. He was the purest form of traveller who survived by living totally off his environment.

Most of us, including myself could not travel in this way. Well, not intentionally anyway. I travel lightweight but not *that* lightweight. I need at least a few essentials and a well-maintained, dependable bike. Being stranded with a broken bike in the middle of nowhere means nothing to the natural traveller – it is just another adventure and something, or somebody, would be bound to come along. That is not really for me though, I am not quite so optimistic – I need to know that I can cycle out of any tight spot and am carrying enough of the right sort of gear to survive any situation; be it a border check-point in some Third World war zone, or a downpour on a remote Welsh hillside.

The bike, and equipment carried, has obviously to be good and trustworthy, but these are not the most important parts of the expedition equation. The most vital component is the adventurer himself or herself. Basically there are a few extra things prospective ATB explorers will need to have before they set out on their dream machines into the uncertainties of foreign or strange lands – they will need to have guts, determination and a certain rashness of spirit. Buying the bike and fitting it out for a trans-Amazonian expedition is one thing. Actually setting out and completing the thing is another. However, you will only get the experience if you go out there and do it. I started out like everybody else – I knew nothing but was willing to learn by continual trial and error. I soon realised that the most difficult part of my inaugural trip had been plucking up the courage to start in the first place – from then on in it became easier as each day passed.

It is the get up and go and the conviction to see things through to the end that really counts. Having lots of money for expenses, being wonderfully fit or possessing muscles are secondary. The last two will come once on the tour anyway. The first one comes from either luck or graft; but it is not always necessary. The major outlay once out into the back of beyond is for food, after all, the means of transport is yourself, so this comes free and food outside Europe can be extremely cheap. To be an expeditionist you need to have the ability to recognise package tours to Torremelinos for what they are – holidays but not travel; you have not really

The loaded up machine.

left Britain behind you on an 18–30 jaunt, you have just transplanted it on to your destination. The desire to do something different, something truly adventurous, is what makes the armchair expeditionist into the real thing – the latter-day hero/heroine of the glossy cycle mags.

An 'expedition' in a narrow sense, normally means some well-staffed trip to the Himalayas or the like. Cycle expeditions on the other hand are usually undertaken on a much more modest scale. Most cyclists choose to keep it simple and travel in pairs. Yet others make it even simpler and go solo, and for various reasons this is how I have normally ventured. Solo not because of any antisocial tendencies but just the need to journey with nobody else to depend upon or have dependent upon me. Many years ago I started travelling solo because I did not know anybody crazy enough who had a couple of years to spare or who fancied accompanying me to the Middle East. I did not particularly want to travel solo, it was simply forced upon me by dint of circumstance.

Solitary travelling, as well as having some nasty drawbacks – such as having nobody to turn to when the going gets really tough – does have many points in its favour. For a start you can go where you want to go – there is nobody else to ask if you want to detour into uncharted territory – a partner may want to play safe and make the next village before nightfall. Compromise may develop your diplomatic skills but it does not get you off the beaten track to where *you* want to go. This may seem selfish but at least you are not upsetting anyone else by your decision. It is also a lot easier to meet people if you are on your own. The local people, or other travellers, will be much more forthcoming to a lone traveller. On the other hand, because I look so young I was once held up at the Turkish–Syrian border because the check-point guards could not believe somebody that baby-faced would be travelling without his parents!

A pair, or a whole team, have each other's company for entertainment and so tend to be somewhat introspective and can sometimes give out 'bad vibes', as it were, to strangers. I have travelled in a pair a few times and whilst it can be fun to share all the various experiences encountered *en route* you do tend to feel alienated from the countryside and the people. Maybe that is only me, however – other people can only truly enjoy a landscape and the like, if there is somebody else to share it with them. There are no hard and fast rules, although travelling in a group of more than four can become very imposing. The group becomes a mobile village on wheels moving through an alien landscape, instead of travellers trying to learn from, and enjoy, their environment. Travelling solo by bike is always rewarding – tough sometimes too but I have never regretted a single trip I have done. Each one has generated further experiences to be added to my personality.

Despite my comments above, touring with partners can be just as rewarding, although in different ways. For instance it can be satisfying to work as a team, to get each other over the bad spots and to come together in the pleasures of a trip. However, travellers must try to stay open-minded about the places they are cycling through and they should not cut off any potential feedback from their destination by becoming introspective between themselves. On my trips with other people – fewer, it must be admitted, than trips I have done by myself – I try to absorb the culture around me instead of imposing myself on it. This is the only way I can describe the feeling of empathy you must develop with the people you meet and the land you will be journeying through.

My expedition to Zambia and Botswana was the most testing one so far. Not so much because of any dangers – perceived or real – or any tough terrain to tackle, but more because the poverty and degradation of the indigenous of the indigenous peoples was hard to bear. The trip was undertaken with Gil Bor, a Californian-based Israeli, whom I had met four years previously in Jerusalem. We went out to cycle in the Kalahari desert. We, as 'rich' Westerners, had not really prepared ourselves for the poverty we were to encounter. To show what I mean I will recount the story in full.

Two male cyclists dismounted wearily from their dusty mountain bikes. They leaned them carefully against a crumbling wall which formed part of a large building with a cross on the top of it. Both cyclists were wearing baggy shorts and long-sleeved cotton shirts and both looked somewhat dishevelled. A few cuts were evenly-distributed on their legs; and socks that were once white, but were now a shade of grey, had

the odd fleck of blood as unintended decoration.

To themselves they look completely normal. To the Irish nun however, who answered the door at the Catholic mission where the two had leaned their machines, they looked very much the opposite. The sight of two sunburned cyclists appearing from the middle of nowhere, in a remote area of southern Africa that had never before seen tourists of any kind, was enough to render the nun speechless for a good few seconds. She looked them up and down, eventually gathered her thoughts and then came out with the classic line of 'Oh, my goodness, have you had an accident?'

Gil and I must have looked a bit dirty but as we had bathed in the Zambesi river the night before we certainly did not think we looked like

Gil and the Sioma missionary nuns.

survivors from a tropical air crash. Her remark did make us take stock of ourselves though and sure enough we were not exactly dressed for the Ritz. No matter how smart we looked when we started off in the mornings, after two hours of pedalling through African dirt we became covered with many layers of fine Kalahari dust. At this point we were actually many hundreds of miles away from the Kalahari Desert but the Kalahari dust gets everywhere in southern Africa. We were cycling through the Western Province of Zambia – an undeveloped area that is extremely sensitive militarily. For some reason we had been granted special military permits to gain access to this area. We had expected to be turned away at the Army head-quarters in Livingstone but to our surprise the powers that be were so bemused by our strange request to take bicycles in that they gave us the required permission after only a few hours. To the best of our knowledge we were the first ever white cycle tourists in this half of the poverty-stricken Western Province and if the missionary nuns at Sioma were right, we were also the first actual tourists!

The nun who greeted us took pity on us and invited us into the mission to meet the other nuns. They sat us down, plied us with hot tea, warm bread and Christmas cake and asked us, wide-eyed, about our trip. In between mouth-fuls of the delicious fare we tried to tell them our story. We told them with great poignancy of our food intake during the last few days and as this seemed to elicit a great deal of sympathy, with the result that more food was placed before us, we told them some more.

Despite their poverty most of the Zambians we met were cheerful.

The Western Province is extremely poor. Malnutrition is common and most of the little kids have big, bloated stomachs. It was tough to dispel the notion that they were well-fed because, despite appearances, they were half-starved. The people live on what they grow – and this is not much. Maize meal, or mealie meal (a coarse form of cornflour) is the staple diet and as this was all we could get our 'rich' western hands on, we had to treat it as our staple diet as well. After a month in Africa I lost a great deal of weight through muscle wastage and stomach upsets. For us it was an experience, for the locals it is their life. We had the nuns to feed us up, the people just have themselves and their few meagre crops. At times it was heartbreaking to pass through small settlements where we knew for a fact that the people only ate one small meal a day. But there was little we could do to alleviate their suffering and this hurt.

Despite their poverty most of the Zambians we met were cheerful and, as seeing us seemed to make them happier, our consciences were somewhat salved. For me, trips abroad are all about meeting people. I think that is why I travel by bike – it is so easy to start a conversation with total strangers. The bicycle is an instant topic of conversation – especially so in the developing countries where they are seen purely as 'native transport' – white men go by car, not bike! Part of the appeal of remote areas, such as deserts or out-of-the-way places in rural Africa, is that the people who live there

Sometimes the Zambesi River had to be crossed by makeshift canoe – not an experience I would like to repeat.

have not seen that many white people. It is a great honour for them to invite us into their homes and, of course, we are greatly honoured by their hospitality. Yet whilst all we can be is little more than five-minute anthropologists, at least we glimpse a culture so very different to our own. This is quite an experience and one I would recommend to anybody who wants to understand and empathise with 'alien' cultures.

The original intention of the trip had been to cycle in the Kalahari Desert and meet the various inhabitants there. Gil, however, had been refused entry to Botswana as he is an Israeli, even though he was told in America that Botswana would not require a visa. He was even arrested for a night to stop him trying to gain entry by other means. The next day after much deliberation I decided I would do part of the planned trip by myself. The dirt tracks of the northern Kalahari were very easy to cycle upon and I reached some extremely remote villages where I was greeted like royalty. However, because Gil and I had split our gear, I was without proper tools and spares so eventually I had to cut short the Kalahari section and after a week I met back up with Gil.

After looking at a large scale map of Zambia, the Western Province seemed to be one of the most remote areas around and so naturally we pointed the bikes in that direction. Much of Africa is pretty dull but this part of Zambia is far from dull. Unlike the Kalahari a few hundred miles to the south, the Western Province is green and lush. The track we cycled on, and which eventually twisted its way past the nuns mission at Sioma, followed the mighty Zambesi River upstream. Certainly if this area had been anywhere else other than on the border between Namibia and Angola then the tourists would have been here long before. There are sights here worthy of any in Africa and we had them all to ourselves.

The terrain we passed was stunningly beautiful and with hippos splashing in the waters a few metres to our right, elephants roaming all around and the spoor of lions being frequently spotted, Zambia really felt like the Africa of our imaginations. Nuns may not feature very frequently in the stereotypical African vista but as two ravenous cyclists, we were extremely glad they were there. There was, however, always a feeling of guilt that because we were Westerners we received preferential treatment – we were fed, the Africans were not. Travel in Third World countries is usually the most exciting thing you can do with an expedition mountain bike but do not expect to come back as the same person. The abject poverty you will undoubtedly see will alter your whole perception of life.

When I am in the Third World I am seen to be extremely rich, in other words I have enough money to be able to buy the amount of food for a day that an African would eat in a week. Yet back in this country I would be considered poor if all I could afford to pay for is a few groceries. In Britain, more often than not, I am seriously in debt – each time I go away I top this debt up and I suppose I am still paying for trips that took place years ago. This does not worry me excessively as I would rather suffer perceived deprivations over here than have to count the pennies and realise I cannot actually afford to gallivant around the world. My trips always mean an awful lot to me. They teach me about myself. I can spot my weaknesses, my faults and my bad points. However, on the flip side, I can also identify my good points. Travelling with a partner will usually be better if these good and bad points are mirror-opposites to each other. Efficient team-work can then come into play; I am awful at making camp-fires, Gil was brilliant; I am good at talking myself out of potentially embarrassing or dodgy situations, Gil usually became lost for words and soon floundered. Parts of his personality complemented the weaker parts of mine and vice versa. Our southern Africa trip was a revelation to us – we saw each other's faults but could compensate for them by offering different skills and personality traits.

To round off this chapter I will relate to you, in narrative form, the different ways both Gil and I coped with a difficult part of our trip. This episode lasted just a day yet it seemed to sum up our whole attitude to the way danger adds a certain something to a trip.

Usually Gil never appeared scared, frightened or nervous – all but once that is. On one day his defences dropped and I saw him scared (or, as he later put it, 'tense'). This was anything but a reassurance for me – after all if he was worried then there must be something wrong – something out of the ordinary.

It was a thunderstorm. African thunderstorms are particularly vicious, and are usually menacing and as dangerous alike to man, beast and landscape. A lightning strike can blast two cyclists into a thousand and one pieces – mangled and charred trees were a vivid testimony to this powerful phenomenon and unfortunately they were not a rarity. Evidence of lightning strikes were all too common and many of the locals had told us tales of whole cattle kraals, with twenty unsuspecting bovines contained therein, being wiped out in a second. Gil was most worried about the fact that we were now cycling across savannah-type terrain where even the singular, skeleton-like trees were few and far between. There was nothing to offer protection against the elements. On the huge Matabele floodplain we were the tallest things around. Riding on rubber tyres was no consolation either – we knew that if one of us was struck that would be it. Also of course help would be many miles away and would anyway be spectacularly unequipped for such emergencies – we would have been lucky to find a village herbalist, never mind a paramedical team experienced in the treatment of burns. This, after all, was rural Africa. And furthermore, as the nuns had told us, no tourists of any kind had ventured this far into Zambia's militarily-sensitive Western Province. We were on our own, and vulnerable.

The storm hit once we were well into treeless terrain and well away from any form of habitation. There was no turning back. We just had to pray and pedal onwards for another couple of hours until we reached the comparative safety of Senanga. This was a small settlement where the dirt-track ended and a pock-marked road took over, and where hopefully the banana trees would deflect the lightning. Or so we hoped, anyway. The actual storm in progress was like some magnificently staged *Son et Lumière* extravaganza replete with a bank of huge multi-dimensional projectors shooting out graphic flashes of forked lightning and a gargantuan set of quadraphonic speakers booming out expansive explosions of thunder as if there were no tomorrow.

All around us shafts of lightning were released every twenty seconds or so. This was

The aftermath of an African thunderstorm. Gil does not look too happy!

followed, most ominously, by thunderclaps that shattered on one side of the head, reverberated angrily over the top and then exploded terrifyingly into the opposite ear, finally tapering off into a long rumble that ushered in the next display. The whole cacophony then started afresh. Each performance seemed to better the last and no matter how complacent we became to the first few bangs, the final explosion always scared us witless. For three seconds the whole sky seemed ready to collapse and the atmosphere became cold and evil. A strange smell reached our nostrils and we began to notice how heavily it was raining. Of course the rain was unlike anything ever experienced in temperate climates. It came down in sheer torrents and with such an intensity that it just about succeeded in ripping the very clothes from our backs. The drops all merged into one single, horizontal battering ram and I am sure that if we had not been wearing tough cotton sun hats we would have been beaten senseless.

After just a few minutes the sandy track filled with creamy, pink rain-water and what was once a cycleable surface became little better than a stream. Progress was further hampered by the gooey sand sucking our fat-tyres into its reddish depths. Pedalling was therefore rather difficult and only just on the feasible side of impossible. In parts, the track became completely waterlogged and we had to ride the bikes gingerly into the deep puddles, trying not to fall off and thereby fully submerging both ourselves and the pannier bags. The water came half-way up the bags anyway so any inhibitions soon left us and our bikes took on a submarine character all of their own (nothing was dry that evening, of course).

The only signs of life, in this huge panorama of landscape, sky and storm, apart from two mad cyclists, were the odd few mottled frogs crossing from one side of the track to the other. They would hop happily from one water-filled footprint to another, and then for some strange reason, once they reached their goal, they repeated the process.

It is little wonder that witchcraft and belief in the animistic spirits of nature can still have a hold over the African peoples, despite the continuous efforts of missionaries to wean them away to the white man's religion. Even a Westerner would need little prompting to believe that this overly dramatic display of nature's wrath was being controlled from without by some malevolent storm god, high up on yonder. We just hoped this African Thor didn't have our names next on his list!

To lessen my chances of being struck I deliberately kept my head lower than Gil's and tried to keep a safe distance away from his spinning back wheel. I also made continuous contingency plans for when Gil was fried to a crisp. Help for him would be useless so I had decided to leave his charred body as it was, prop up a bike as a protective conductor and then lie down flat until the storm passed. Unpleasant thoughts maybe, and cowardly ones at that, but at least it kept my mind off thinking what would happen if the lightning preferred to discharge into me instead. Such morbid thoughts are natural though, and so I ran through in my mind's eye just exactly what a strike would feel like, if, indeed, I would feel anything at all. I also tried to initiate a preview of the movie clips of my life flashing before me. What would I look like afterwards? What would people's reaction be back at home? The hypothetical answers were pretty discouraging.

Whilst rain beat all around and lightning shafts struck here, there and everywhere and resounding booms of thunder echoed throughout the whole sky, I kept my thoughts as occupied as possible. I even composed mind drafts of a really thrilling end to a book chapter I was going to write! I still knew, however, that no matter how much I tried to dispel the notion, a single discharge of electricity into my body would evaporate such thoughts instantly. I seemed to be able to generate a form of Dutch courage by thinking of the worst possible outcomes and speculating on how ridiculous it all sounded. Basically such thinking was all that could be done. The storm was way beyond our conscious control. What would happen would happen, no matter how 'protected' we thought we were. Pedalling on slowly but surely seemed to be the only sensible option. Stopping may have been worse – possibly a stationary object would be more likely to be hit? Or maybe not – but we were not hanging around to find out.

Imperceptibly the storm receded, the dramatic special effects died away and just a steady drizzle remained. The fear and worry lifted. The danger, real or imagined, was past and within minutes it felt silly to even think it had ever existed. Gil turned to me and admitted he had been 'tense'. I said nothing but felt incredibly good as we strained onwards to Senanga – sodden but safe.

# VIEWPOINTS

*Why do you tour on a mountain bike?*

**Nigel Jackson** 'I really believe that the mountain bike has earned the tag 'the ultimate expedition machine' – a bike that can go anywhere that a touring bike can, with little or no more effort. But for me, the real fun starts where a touring bike is forced to stop. A mountain bike can traverse terrain where it would firstly be impossible or foolhardy to try and ride a conventional tourer and secondly where it would probably cause terminal damage if it were possible to stay on. This could be anywhere from poorly maintained Third World roads or jeep tracks, through to complete wilderness areas where no roads exist at all.'

*What are your basic reasons for wanting to travel in the first place?*

**Nigel Jackson** 'A growing dissatisfaction with the 'nine to five' existence which I was leading, and was in danger of becoming ensnared in permanently if some radical changes were not forthcoming, coupled with the idea that there was a big wide world out there, and it was about time that I got out and had a look at some of it.'

# 8 Mountain Bike Racing for Fun and for Profit

(Fat-Tyre Flying)

There are basically three things you can do with your mountain bike – commute with it, tour with it or race with it. Commuting is an end unto itself and can be an enormous amount of fun. Dodging cars and buses is a pastime that involves a lot of risk and depending on how you ride, a fifteen minute commuting journey into work, school, college or wherever can have as much adventure packed into it as the most dramatic Spielberg film imaginable!

Touring, as you will already have gathered, is my favourite way of employing the mountain bike. The excitement of travel in strange lands, or in strange places somewhat closer to home, soon becomes an addiction and without a regular 'fix' of adventure travel – whether it be yearly, monthly or weekly – I start to wilt. However, neither commuting nor touring are the activities mountain bikes were created for. They were designed, rather, for racing down

Cars are not always the fastest things on the street.

hillsides. The human being is a compulsively competitive creature, so it comes as no big surprise to learn that in Marin County, California (a location known for its fair share of eccentrics) a mutant fat-tyred bike evolved from a cross between a Schwinn paper-boy bike and a lightweight racer – it could take the rider downhill in a fashion and at a speed most people would consider as suicidal. These speedy downhills could be bettered by more daring or more skilful, riders. The race was on. . .

With the addition of gears they could race uphill too. A new sport was born. Many people see racing on mountain bikes as somehow aberrant – an activity to be looked down upon with pity and disgust. Yet mountain biking was developed, matured and spread out to the rest of the world because of the competitive urge that manifested itself on the makeshift race tracks of Californian dirt hillsides. Racing today, and on this side of the Atlantic, is a little bit further on than simply choosing to go hell for leather down a measured section of dirt. Race devotees have a number of offshoots from pure downhilling to consider.

The most popular types of event for the riders themselves are the long course races. These can sometimes be held in wilderness areas, will tend to be for the very fit only because of the mileage involved and whilst they will offer intrepid spectators a good view, for the more valley-based viewers there is little to see except the frenetic start and the mud-splattered finish. For this reason it is the short course races that spectators most enjoy. All the action is concentrated on a tight circuit that the riders will lap many times. Water splashes, artificial bumps and short but steep descents may be built in for added excitement. Television cameras can often be enticed to such events which are usually held within easy reach of civilisation. Television has often shied away from the wilderness courses because of the logistics of getting the cameras there.

Observed trials, where the rider pits his or her skills not against other riders specifically but against a marked out and tremendously difficult set of obstacles, has a small but devoted following in this country. Spectators generally have a good time if the riders are in any way inept because the chances of crashes are proportionately higher compared to the other types of events listed above. Spills are commonplace but so are skills and if you have never watched really adept exponents of trials riding, handling mountain bikes like they were welded to the bike then try and get yourself along to a local trial. Most of them are held down south; with the Wendover Bash, organised by Geoff Apps of the Cross-country Cycling Club, being the most well known. Some events are often

The Orange team van.

held over a whole weekend and are just as much a social gathering as a means of rubbing your opponents' faces into the ground. They include all three types of competition – the Kielder Classic based up in Northumberland attracts nearly four hundred riders and is one such event where it is not just out and out speed that is tested.

One further type of competition which is gaining in favour – especially with the converts from parallel outdoor disciplines – is mountain bike orienteering. In such competitions it can often be brains that win over brawn – routes across rough terrain have to be studied and evaluated and the shortest route around a course may not be the most efficient one. Good mountain and navigation skills are inculcated by such events and so perform a very useful function.

There are always many events being organised up and down the country of all the different persuasions. Unlike a couple of years ago when there was a dearth of competition and a racer's diary was not exactly overflowing with weekends away, the problem now is which event out of the multitude should you go for. Some are more prestigious than others – this can be because the event is well established or possibly because the purse (prize-list) is bigger. There is nothing like a large prize for enticing racers to ride a particular event. Despite races being organised and executed left, right and centre there are still gaps around the country where there is a conspicuous lack of regular competitions. The south-east is over-subscribed with events; Wales – given its size, has hardly any, and likewise Scotland is still a novelty destination for many riders. There are other, though less well-known, gaps throughout the country and without access to transport, money and accommodation many mountain bikers eager to pit their calf muscles against erstwhile opponents may be missing out.

One answer could be for the hapless, raceless rider to organise his or her own event – for women this could be especially relevant. Women-only races would boost the popularity of the sport amongst, what some people call, the 'weaker sex' (although any man who has seen a rider such as Deb Murrell pass him would rapidly reconsider such a definition). To organise an event you initially have to gain access to a large area of land which should have no public rights of way crossing it (*see* Chapter 3) – so go and ask a landowner if you can borrow his meadow and woodland for a day or two. Secondly, you should make sure you buy adequate insurance cover in case of accidental injuries or damage. Both of these may cost quite a lot of money and organising events can take up a lot of time and effort. If you are still serious about staging an event contact either the Mountain Bike Club or the Cross-country Cycling Club. Both organisations are past experts in such matters and can offer help, advice and encouragement.

Most events in the UK attract two types of rider – there is a hard core of serious racers but the rest are there just to go round what may be a satisfying and punishing course in the presence of like-minded, casually orientated fellows. The riders who do it for fun admire the casual side to mountain biking – a sport that has, as yet, few rules. This lack of regulations is to be applauded but there are some who would like to see the sport adopt a more professional attitude (in other words more rules and regulations). The majority prefer to see it carry on in its haphazard fashion, bereft of people telling riders what to do, what to wear and other such stipulations.

Mountain biking has not been monopolised by the élite yet – races are still open to everybody and the courses are not yet so long and arduous as to mean rank amateurs cannot enjoy them – this may change however. Unfortunately I can see mountain biking going the way of other sports which have been systematically

In some races riding the bike is not always possible.

regulated out of existence and have also been taken over by the élite. All the fun, risks and devil-may-care attitudes are gradually wiped out and the sport ceases to be quite so open and welcoming.

Because of this drift towards so-called professionalism I tend to echo the sentiments of Max Glaskin and Jeremy Torr, who, in their book *Mountain Biking* (*see* Further Reading section), have this to say about the future of mountain bike racing, 'Whereas other cycle sports are chained by laws which have stultified their growth and development, mountain biking revels in the luxury of doing exactly what it pleases. . . . The day that mountain biking gets tied down by its own laws is the day to hang up your saddle.'

# EQUIPMENT FOR RACING

As with expeditions there are an assortment of necessities that the racer will need before he or she starts to compete and like expeditioning this assortment cannot always be bought over the counter. A race-ready bike, a helmet, a pair of shades, a multi-coloured skin suit, a tool-kit, a pump and puncture repair kit can be acquired quite easily if you have got the money. The attributes of a racer – or at least the potential to get them – are harder to gain. So if you have not got huge stores of stamina, a lot of guts, and legs of burnished steel then you may not be the next Joe Murray! Training may develop these attributes but if you have not got the inbuilt will to win then no amount of the above three will get you around a race circuit in the fastest time. A single-minded mental attitude is so important that the lack of it will mean certain failure.

You may have this killer instinct to be the best, so what do you need to buy as an aspiring racer to be able to test your animal tendencies out on other racers? Bike choice is an obvious first step. If you are still riding around on a tatty

Toe-clips are essential for serious racers.

old Dawes Ranger then you may be in the market for a more up-to-date bike. Dawes, to their credit, have improved their new bikes which no longer ride uphill like plodding camels, nor downhill like marauding tanks. They are nifty and if their 'laid back' geometry suits you then they have some useful models to choose from. However, if you have about £500 to spend you can get race-ready machines that will have 'steeper' frame angles than the Dawes bikes and which come fully equipped for fast action. Long reach stems will force you into a low-slung riding position and short back ends will power you to the top of the steepest of slopes – if you have the legs and the energy for it that is.

Standard bikes compete just as well with the custom ones – it is the rider, not the bike, that wins races. There are now hundreds of bikes to choose from – some are far better than others for racing on – you will have to try some out for

Custom built race bikes can perform wonders.

Shimano produce the best gears for racing
mountain bikes. The new Rapidfire gear set-up is
ideal for racers.

The Tip Top puncture repair kit.

size to see if they fit your riding style. Most
mountain bikes now being sold are racing
models, most come equipped with the unbeat-
able Shimano groupsets, most will have very
similar geometries and most will be very expensive! If you are serious about being faster than
your fellows however, cost will not matter all
that much, and if you are very fast you may be
picked for one of the trade teams and will get
your bikes free and all the expenses that racing
incurs, paid for courtesy of your sponsor!

Aside from the bike and the obvious tool-kit
and puncture repair kit (the Tip Top one with
carbon dioxide canisters included is ideal for
racers) and possibly a spare inner tube or two
the aspiring racer should also invest in some

form of eye protection and some type of helmet.
Helmets are obligatory at races anyway, but are
also trendy so they may also be worn when the
rider is not racing. Sun-glasses are not essential, nor are they obligatory but they can literally
be a real eye-opener when it comes to competitions. No longer will a stiff breeze, or the draft
generated by speed, be a handicap – the eyes
can be protected by a bit of wraparound
Perspex.

In the wilderness and at speed, rocks,
branches, gullies and other such obstacles can
appear out of nowhere to knock about both the
rider and the machine. If you can break sturdy
bikes on offending obstacles such as these you
can be sure that you could also break your head.

And likewise for short course events and trials, where similar and possibly more numerous obstacles can leap out at unsuspecting riders – the unhatted ones suffer concussion when their head hits hard ground; the hatted ones simply get a bit of a headache. Of course, wearing a helmet is sometimes uncomfortable and even in temperate conditions they can restrict heat loss from the head. The foam sweat-bands inside the helmet soak up perspiration and now and then the bands reach saturation point when all the stored up water is released and runs over the back of the head and the face. This is funny to watch from afar but disconcerting for the wearer – especially if it happens mid-race!

Helmets rarely sit on one's head with too much precision unless tightened to a painful degree. In general most people wear helmets

Helmets and eye-shields are *de rigeur* for active mountain bikers.

too big for their heads and fail to keep them secured tightly enough. This may be more comfortable but in the first serious crash the helmet will be thrown aside or pushed off. Helmets for racers are not a fashion accessory, they are an insurance against injury, so ensure they are secure. The choice in styles, weights and 'fittings' nowadays is quite impressive – no doubt influenced by the American market and the triathlon scene. Choosing a helmet can be difficult because of this variety, but then again most bike shops only sell a couple of different makes so the choice will be, in effect, easier. Unless you know your exact head size it would be unwise to buy a helmet from a mail-order catalogue – you need to check the fit of the helmet and this cannot be done by guessing, so always go to a shop for such purchases. With the help of a bike shop assistant find the helmet that feels the most snug and the most comfortable. Strap one on and then wobble it about to see the amount of play there is. Experiment with the Velcro foam pads that are supplied with most helmets. If the helmet moves easily and does not take the scalp with it then it is either too big or not correctly adjusted.

When mountain biking, a falling cyclist may collide with small rocks and so forth and so the leather lattice-work helmets favoured by the racing fraternity (the 'bunch of bananas type' hat) would be too open and therefore unsafe. Likewise the aerodynamic teardrop helmets would serve no real purpose out in the wilds – even if it is blowing a force nine gale – and they do not offer the same degree of all-round protection that the standard Bell-type helmets offer. Modern designs have been developed over many years and the helmets of today are both lightweight and extremely strong. They have to pass stringent safety standards – the most commonly encountered is the American ANSI Z 90.4 where the test procedure is to drop the weighted helmet onto hard ground from a height of one metre. Most helmets

Protective head gear is obligatory for races – but looks good anyway!

not however, mean a huge drop in the effectiveness of the protection offered; instead of the polycarbonate shell absorbing the impact and shattering, the polystyrene crushes on impact and this destruction therefore absorbs the force. The polystyrene foam has to be held in place by a Lycra-Spandex cover for this reason – it does not conform to the safety standards if the cover is not used. As with all helmets the ultralights have to be replaced after a serious crash but as they usually crumble on impact this is easier to realise.

This type of helmet does not come cheap – but then again nothing does in mountain biking – so think carefully before buying one. Are you really going to be racing a lot and are you really going to be pushing yourself and the bike to the limits? If you are planning to do neither then wearing a helmet is by no means compulsory. Wearing one will, however, mark you out as an aware and 'with-it' mountain biker; if you have all the other bits and bobs, then a helmet and a good pair of shades will top the image off nicely.

Being able to see clearly, and to effectively act upon received visual information, is incredibly important in the sport of mountain biking. When you consider that in a typical sortie through a local patch of woodland the average mountain biker has to avoid a whole host of possible injury-inducing obstacles – tree branches, tree roots, undulations, radical undulations (holes), fallen logs, squirrels and so forth – then it is obvious that any impairment of the vision can be somewhat dangerous. Basically this is a long-winded way of saying that you should wear eye-protection. It could be just as important as wearing a helmet (and just as trendy of course!).

Blocking off the light by wearing sun-glasses makes eyes light-sensitive and long-term damage can result. A vitamin D deficiency may also occur if insufficient daylight reaches the retina. However, sun-glasses are useful on a bike – and ten times more so on a mountain

either meet or exceed these requirements, but do not buy from 'dodgy' shops just in case they bought in a load of untested imports. A few helmets also pass the Snell safety standard which involves a more realistic drop of two metres. The British mark of approval is the BS6863 standard. All of the standards ensure helmets will protect the wearer to a high degree – that is, if they are correctly fitted.

The trendiest thing to be seen around in at the moment is the shell-less helmet. This type of hard hat (the ultralight) dispenses with the polycarbonate outer shell and is simply a polystyrene block. This saves an impressive amount of weight; for instance the average hard shell helmet weighs about fourteen to sixteen ounces whilst the ultralights weigh a negligible seven to eight ounces. This loss in weight does bike. Mud, stones and other material is being flung up continuously, and insects do seem to have a habit of aiming straight at open eyes whenever you are nearing a really tricky downhill section. Eye protection in these situations can be quite a boon. If the day is sunny and bright, sun-glasses can also be useful in filtering out glare and unwanted ultraviolet rays. If, on the other hand, the day is really overcast, sun-glasses can often be converted into clear eye-shields instead. Or, if you have money to spend, another option could be to buy a replacement 'yellow' or 'peach' lens which enhances low-light conditions and increases definition. I have been wearing Oakley's fitted with yellow lenses for a while now and they are excellent – a grey day in Lancashire appears like a sunny day in Lanzarote!

# THE CROSS CROSS-OVER

One interesting development over the last two seasons has been the apparent cross-fertilisation between traditional cycle sport and mountain bike racing. For instance, Chris Young, Tim Davies, David Baker, Tim Gould, Kevin Sabiston and others have all moved over from cyclo-cross; and Neil Martin, the former Emmelle/MBK professional road racer has come over from the discipline of road racing. This works the other way round too – John Tomac has taken up road racing, Carl Sturgeon is doing well at Crits and Paul Skilbeck is taking up cyclo-cross. Instead of all the disciplines competing to win the favours of aspiring speed cyclists all three are mixing together – mountain biking is merging ever so slightly into the mainstream.

It could be argued however, that what started out as a Messianic movement of reform and originality has come back on itself and has bastardised many of its original ideals. Races have become more professional, racers are now more single-minded and committed, more commercial money is being pumped into the sport and, because of this, the sport gets a higher profile – but a profile that is all about racing. All this professionalism is possibly inevitable but it is not welcomed by everybody and the least I can do for the dissenters is to sound a few warning bells.

Professionalism may be good in the long run for manufacturers and so forth but the amateurish, haphazard aspect of the sport was one of the reasons people were first attracted to mountain bike racing. There were no rules set down for competing, no special clothes had to be worn, bikes could be flamboyant or boring, helmets could be worn or not, nobody really lost any races because it was taking part that mattered. Stopping mid-way through a race for a cigarette was not unusual and would not have been seen as wrong. Before 1987 mountain biking was more relaxed and there was a more open, friendly atmosphere at races. If this changes the grassroots support may wither and die. Road racing, however, has long had a 'must win at all costs' type attitude. Bikes had to be standard, clothes had to be plain, restrictions were everywhere and the people were so committed they had little time for anything else but cycle racing. Mountain biking broke the mould – clothing became 'jazzy', bikes became odd and against the whole ideal of stripped down featherweight elegance. Mountain bikers were more sociable, less uptight, more friendly. Yet this golden age was only a few years ago – so what happened, what went wrong? It is hard to say – perhaps nothing went wrong and perhaps where we are today is the best we could ever have hoped for? I somehow doubt it.

A hard core of committed mountain bikers are becoming more and more professional and attitudes are nowhere near as casual as four or five years ago. Today single-mindedness, determination and fitness rule the roost. For many, the amateurishness is a great loss; for others, it

The mass start is popular.

will not be missed in the slightest. Certainly, for mountain biking to continue to prosper, it would seem that the more professional approach will do most for the sport. Big sponsors want a return for their money and a more slick PR job on the part of mountain bike organisers guarantees this return. Many people rejected road racing because of its cliquey nature – many will now be abandoning mountain bike racing. Mountain biking had the potential to be something different – a new type of sport that rejected the ethics of traditional cycle competition. It failed.

However, despite the doom and gloom picture painted above, ATB racing still has a long way to go before it gets as cliquey or as over-organised as British Cycling Federation road racing. It still has the fresh anarchic air of informality. Now no more than a breeze, instead

of a gust, but it still manages to delight those who rejected the road racing scene. Novice or sports riders often still compete on the same course, and at the same time, as the experts. This is still very different to traditional cycle sport events – after all, imagine having a few hundred lesser riders joining in on the *Tour de France!* Rules are still few and far between – the only ones you will encounter are firstly, you must ride on a bona fide mountain bike (with flat handlebars and 1.5in tyres or above); secondly, you must wear a helmet; thirdly, you cannot change your bike if it collapses on you; and finally, you must sign a waiver form saying you take full responsibility for your actions and that you accept the organisers' decisions as final.

Various people within the sport and various organisations from without, would like to 'hijack' mountain biking in order to further their

Racing can be tough.

own ideals and feather their own nests. We are powerless to stop this happening. As a group we are too amorphous and fragmented to be able to put up much of a battle. Even the MBC can do little to combat the bigger bodies coming in and imposing rules. However much they try, the onward drift of progress will attempt to sweep them aside. This is not to say that progress is not a good thing, but mountain bike racing had the potential to journey in a different and less formalistic direction. The progress gained has been at the expense of 'casualness'. The sport has been sanitised and scrubbed too clean – a crying shame, but there is little we can do about it now.

The best we can do is campaign for events to be kept open to as many riders as want to enter and to make sure the racing élite do not close off the sport to lesser riders. The fight is not quite over yet, so perhaps such organisations as the MBC and the CCCC can still hold on to some of the reins of power. If they do not, mountain bike racing will just be a glorified version of cyclo-cross – a road race in the hills completed by élites and watched by lesser mortals. This is exactly what many of the early mountain bikers in this country were rebelling against – it is strange what the passage of time can do to an activity!

The racers competing today are a fine bunch of people – most have the good of mountain biking at heart. However, the sport is in danger of being diluted by the various outside bodies who want to grab a slice of the action. Four hundred people can turn up to compete at mountain bike events with each one paying upwards of £5 to enter. Similar numbers do not turn up at the meetings of other cycle competitions. Mountain biking is now so popular that the only way for the outside bodies to contain it is to attempt to incorporate it into their own structures. Despite the reservations above about amateurishness and so forth, I am realistic enough to realise that mountain biking cannot continue in its totally distinct direction.

It is getting too big and unwieldy for that. A governing body is undoubtedly needed – my only hope is that this body will be mountain bike based and not some off-shoot of the traditional cycle-racing organisations. Being affiliated is one thing, being incorporated is another. Racing has a lively future ahead of it – let us hope that it can become 'professional' but at the same time remain 'independent'.

# VIEWPOINTS

*On most courses which do you think would be faster, a mountain bike or a cyclo-cross bike?*

**Tim Davies** 'On the whole you could probably do better on a cyclo-cross bike. Especially on carrying sections and through muddy woods. A mountain bike will always be best for descending though. Downhill you cannot go one hundred per cent or you risk puncturing. You have got to go about eighty or ninety per cent. I prefer cyclo-cross because you get a change of bikes and if something goes wrong it is not the end of the world. If you puncture in a mountain bike race that could cost you the whole race.'

*Where do you see the mountain bike racing scene in a couple of years time?*

**Tim Gould** 'In Britain and Europe it should improve over the next couple of years and then level off. The good races will become established and the poor ones disappear.'

**David Baker** 'It depends on whether the sport sorts itself out, with a governing body and established officials and rules like the other branches of the sport. If it does the potential is there for big improvements.

*Do you think bikes and components will get better and better for racing?*

**Tim Gould** 'The bikes have come on a lot very quickly and it is hard to see where improvements can come from except by weight reduction. I think we will see the weight go down to that of a cross bike. Like the road, people will try different materials for frames and different frame designs, but nothing significant will happen – just gimmicks.'

*Where do you see the British racing scene in a couple of years time?*

**Paul Skilbeck** 'I have no doubt about it. The British MTB scene will be the most competitive and the best organised scene in the world. The type of organisation which is being mooted at the moment (for example the British Mountain Biking Association run by Greg Oxenham of Bike UK/Chainsport) is basically very professional. Obviously I have not studied other models in other countries, but basically the scene needs to get very serious. Now, some of the top cyclo-cross riders and even some of the top road riders are coming in to the sport.'

*But won't this dilute the field, making once prize-winning riders into no-hopers?*

**Paul Skilbeck** 'Well, the answer to that is to have a slightly differently structured prize list – for instance in some races £1000 has been given to the winner and then only £30 for tenth place. However, a far more professional way of doing it would be to have £500 for first prize and then a good amount for twentieth place. For instance with a prize purse of £675 you can have first place getting £100 and fifteenth place getting £25. That will support a professional cycling scene.

My biggest concern is keeping mountain biking afloat and I think that after the great commercial bubble bursts if the sport is not really well entrenched, and there is a really strong grassroots following, it is going to die.

*Mountain biking is very popular right now but is this going to be the biggest mountain biking gets?*

**Lester Noble** 'No, no it's going to get really big.'

*On the par with what?*

**Lester Noble** 'Well, if you look back to motor-cross ten years ago which had regular TV coverage every week I think it could go that way. Racing will always be a small percentage of the mass market but I think mountain biking is just going to keep on growing and growing.'

*What's the future going to be like for mountain bike racing?*

**Matt Mills** 'Over the next couple of years we will see more and more Pro road and cross riders crossing over into mountain bike racing simply because the money is better and the atmosphere more relaxed. I think multi-stage races will also start to spring up, alongside the existing single venue races. Eventually we could see a kind of mountain bike *Tour de France* over a variety of terrain.'

# 9 Custom Bike Building

## ('The Creation of Dreams,' by Dave Yates)

Dave Yates is one of this country's foremost frame builders. As an indicator of his pre-eminence all I need to mention is that he exports his custom machines to clients in America! By and large British frame builders are the best in the world. To demonstrate why this is the case it would be necessary to ride a custom bike built by one of the top two UK mountain bike builders. So, a rider having a go on either a Roberts or a Dave Yates machine would notice quite a difference in the feel of the ride and the sheer quality of the frame finishing. Not an ugly rippled joint in sight! The second best way to demonstrate the above would be for Dave Yates himself to talk us through how he creates frames from scratch; this we have:

The term custom frame can mean many things to many people. The interpretation can vary from changing the colour scheme on a mass-produced frame to a minutely-detailed specification covering materials, dimensions, and finish. The frame featured in this chapter is my own personal frame, built to fit myself and my style of riding. The requirement was for reliability, 'sensible' geometry, super climbing ability and something different for pose value!

The first is obvious – it would not look terribly good if my own frame broke. The second is more for purely practical reasons. As I am not going to race or indulge in very steep hill descents I need a 'middle of the road' geometry to do most things reasonably well. The climbing ability of a frame appears to be directly related to the rear centre length (the distance from the centre of the bottom bracket to the centre of the wheel). I wanted to try this out for myself to see if it really worked. The last requirement was purely due to the fashion conscious nature of the mountain bike market – I needed something radical enough to double as a 'company demonstrator' for at least a year to eighteen months until the mass market showed signs of catching up. At about the fifth attempt at a design I came across an article in the American magazine *Mountain Bike Action* featuring the Nishiki Alien with its chainstays over the chainset. I rushed off to the stores to see what could be used to achieve this configuration. I must point out at this stage that our stores hold examples of practically every type and size of quality bicycle tube known to man. My standard procedure when confronted with a frame building problem is to retire to the stores and contemplate the racks! It might not be very scientific but it usually works. Having played with the contents of various boxes I arrived at the following set-up: Reynolds forks, Columbus Max O.R. main triangle, Reynolds bracing tube, Tange Prestige rear stays. This, I felt, would give resilience at the front end coupled with a stiff rear triangle.

The larger diameter of the Columbus tubes ovalised across the plane of the frame would give good support to the bottom bracket shell in the absence of conventional chainstays. The only extra tube is the eight or so inches of cross brace. The use of Tange Prestige fork blades in the wishbone rear stay design adds weight but is incredibly stiff.

I approach all custom frame design along the same lines – apart from dimensions, the most

Mitreing.

important factor to be considered is 'what will the frame be used for'. I tend to spend some time discussing with the customer his or her motivation and intentions and then build up a picture of the eventual use that the finished bicycle will be put to. The end result is a combination of common sense, sound engineering principles, and experience. The following photographs show how the frame is built once the design process has been completed.

## Mitreing

The secret of any joint in any well-built frame is the fit of the two pieces of tube one to the other. With round tubes I use an attachment for the lathe to machine-mitre the tube end. Columbus Max O.R. is ovalised at each end of the tube so the mitreing has to be done the hard way. I use the linisher (belt sander) to rough out the joint then finish with a file.

The nearly finished mitre.

## The Nearly Finished Mitre

This is the top tube to seat tube joint in its final position. All that remains is to clean off the rag on the top tube and give the whole joint area a good clean with eighty grit-abrasive cloth. Cleanliness is imperative to obtain a sound joint as braze will not stick to grease or oxide.

## Positioning the Tubes

This type of frame (lugless) is first assembled in the jig using clamps and so forth to position the tubes in their correct relationship to one another. The jig is adjustable in all directions to allow very fine setting of the frame dimensions. Once the frame is set, the joints are tacked with small amounts of brass in two or three places to hold all the joints in place.

## Bronze Welding

Because of the nature of this frame I did the joints one section at a time – seat tube to bottom bracket, front triangle, wishbone seat stay arrangement, brace tube and chainstays. This meant that it was taken out of the jig after the front triangle was tacked so that the joints could be finished using the technique of bronze welding. This entails building up a fillet of brass around each joint (in fact the material is silicon bronze but is always known as brass).

## The Rear Wishbone is Tacked into Position

This operation is very tricky. I am making use of the frame builders most frequently used jig here, a piece of bent welding rod! The whole assembly has to be positioned fairly accurately using the spring of the bent rod to hold the parts in place. Then the joints were tacked one at a time with the alignment being checked after each tack.

Positioning the tubes.

Bronze welding.

The rear wishbone is tacked into position.

Starting to look like a frame.

## Starting to Look Like a Frame

The frame is now at a stage where the general outline can be recognised. This view also shows most of the jig. This is based on a heavy steel frame of known truth. The bottom bracket shell is located on a fixture which positions the centre of the shell 100mm from the plane of the jig. The head tube is held by two collars on a mandrel which is also positioned 100mm from the jig by means of setting screws. This means that with the top of the seat tube held on a similar screw set mandrel, the frame can be very accurately set in track. The rear dropouts are held on a dummy axle which is adjustable for both rear-centre distance and bottom bracket drop via scales engraved on the jig frame. The seat angle and head angle are set by means of co-ordinates referenced from a vertical datum through the bottom bracket centre. The whole jig swivels about a vertical and horizontal axis so that each joint can be positioned to best advantage for brazing.

## Brace Tube

Here the tube which will stabilise the seat tube against the chainstay loads is being tacked into place. I have used a piece of 20 gauge 531 tube. I have since discovered that this tube makes a wonderful handle for carrying the bike!

## Marking the Chainstay

In custom frame building the most commonly used measuring devices are the eye and the pen, here being used to mark the chainstay for initial cutting and fitting. My way of working on prototypes such as this does not involve much formal drawing, but relies heavily on holding the

Brace tube.

Marking the chainstay.

piece in place and seeing what it looks like! I must add here that although this style of operation suits me, it does not agree with everyone; each frame builder does it differently.

## Filing the Mitre

This is the technique seen in the previous photograph but further down the road. The initial cut has been made and the laborious job of filing the mitre on the end of the chainstay is about to begin. I am often asked if there is a machine or a tool to do this sort of job. The short answer is no. Other than the linisher seen previously, or a smaller grinder, to take the bulk out, the only way of obtaining the extremely complicated profile of this sort of joint is to file a bit off and see if it fits.

## Welding the Joint

The frame needs to be held in all sorts of positions to get each joint into the best place for

Filing the mitre.

Welding the joint.

bronze welding. To control the molten brass, the joint has to be arranged so that the pool of brass can be worked 'uphill'. This allows the molten brass to be supported by the solidified brass under it.

## *The End is in Sight!*

Here the rear fork end or 'dropout' is being brazed in. Again, notice the job has been positioned to allow best access to the joint. The ends are only finish brazed after checking the alignment with a wheel of known truth. In all the photographs where I am using the torch, the flame can be seen to be very bright. If they were in colour, the flame would be seen to be bright green instead of the more usual blue. This is because I have a gas fluxer fitted, which causes the acetylene to pick up a small amount of liquid flux on its way to the torch from the cylinder. This turns the flame to an incredibly

The end is in sight!

Braze on bits.

bright green, the only remedy for which is cheap blue sun-glasses!

## Braze on Bits

The term 'braze on' is rather misleading, as any frame builder worth his salt will silver solder most of the bits like bottle cage bosses and cable eyes on to the frame. This is to minimise the heat input so that the tube stands less chance of damage. Brass melts at around 850°C, whilst Easyflo silver solder melts at only 610°C. In this shot I am actually marking the position of the bottle cage boss holes.

## Structure

I included this shot because it shows the structure of the rear of the frame quite clearly, showing the bronze welding at each joint. The unconventional nature of the rear stays eliminates 'chain suck' completely as there is nothing for the chain to catch on! This layout also allows a super short rear centre distance which aids climbing considerably. By the way, I am drilling the holes for the bottle bosses.

## Sophisticated Jig

I use a wide range of sophisticated jigs to place the braze-ons in position, most of which bear more than a passing resemblence to pliers and bits of bent tin! When engaged upon custom and prototype work no two jobs are the same so jigs and fixtures tend to get in the way and for the most part are too much hassle. I find the combination of experience, a good eye and a steady hand as fast and as accurate as any other method I have tried.

Structure.

Sophisticated jig.

## A More Sophisticated Jig

Holding the roller-cam pivots in place using a file and a piece of slotted steel, allows them to be positioned very accurately, but allows a certain amount of expansion movement. All the metals used in frame building expand when heated and contract when cooled. One of the secrets of successful frame building is knowing how to allow the metal to move without locking stress into the finished frame. Any jig should be designed to allow the metal to expand and contract without losing its position.

## Grit Blasting

The flux used in brazing is necessary to prevent oxidation of the steel and to dissolve any oxide which does form. Unfortunately, the borax from which the flux is made, ends up like glass over the surface of the joint upon cooling. The most effective way to get rid of this deposit is by grit

A more sophisticated jig.

Grit blasting.

Taking the high spots off the brass with an air-driven linisher.

blasting. The photograph shows the interior of the blasting cabinet. The grit, very fine particles of cast iron, is propelled by compressed air through the nozzle I am holding in my right hand. The grit travels at such a speed that the oxide and flux are stripped off, leaving bare metal. This has to be done before the final filing and polishing of all the joints.

## Finishing Off

This is the bit that sends the cost of a frame like this sky high. Each joint must be filed, scraped and then polished with abrasive cloth. I use an air-driven linisher to take the high spots off the brass. Great care is needed not to take chunks out of the tube – one slip with the linisher and the frame could be ruined. I only use it very

Scraping the profile of the joint to remove the deeper file marks.

Polishing the scraper marks with eighty grit aluminium oxide abrasive cloth.

Forks.

sparingly and sometimes not at all. The profile of the joint is roughed out with a file and then scraped to remove the deeper file marks. At this stage several imperfections usually show up which have to be filled with brass then filed and scraped again. Once I am happy with the profile of the joint I polish the scraper marks out with eighty grit aluminium oxide abrasive cloth. Each joint can take up to an hour. This particular frame took the better part of ten hours to finish off. There was in total approximately thirty-five hours' work that went into this frame by the time it was ready to be assembled into a bicycle.

## Forks

The mechanics of brazing the forks together are exactly the same as for the rest of the frame. This shot shows the jig quite clearly. The vee block holds the steering column, and the dummy axle holds the fork ends which are brazed into

the fork blades first. The clamp is set so that it only just holds the column – this allows for expansion.

## Alignment

It is important that the fork ends are perfectly parallel so the wheel sits correctly in the slots. This tool is used to make sure this is so. It is also used on the rear ends. The items seen on the wall over my left shoulder are some of the jigs used for jobs like brazing the seat tube into the bottom bracket and bending the fork blades.

## Painting the Finished Frame

The paint finish can make or break a frame. If the best frame in the world is painted badly then no one will want it. The reverse is also true! All good quality frames are stove enamelled or in some cases finished with two-pack epoxy paint. The

Alignment.

Painting the finished frame.

The completed custom bike.

latter contains cyanide which is highly poisonous if inhaled, so we do not use it. The painting schedule consists of: etch primer – this keys chemically to the metal surface; colour coats, then stove – sometimes if a complicated finish is being done then more than one stoving is carried out – this is done in an electric oven that can hold ten frames; transfers are applied and allowed to dry over night; clear lacquer is applied over everything and the frame is stoved again. One gleaming ATB frame emerges ready to be assembled into a complete bike.

## The Completed Custom Bike

Here it is – finished and fully tested by Alex Hayles. Custom bikes are all special to the person they are made for – the whole point of such a bike is that it is unique.

So that is how I do it – there are as many different ways of building a frame as there are frame builders and I have always contended that as long as the finished article is right for the job then the method is not critical.

145

# 10 Where Now for the Mountain Bike?

Rest assured the mountain bike is here to stay. It looks set to be the utilitarian bike of the future. As I mentioned in the introduction it is likely that the world and his dog will soon have one. This increase in numbers will bring its own problems – for instance, access could be a major difficulty for off-road cyclists ten years hence. However, access problems aside, the mountain bike boom will continue. Whereas a couple of years ago a mountain biker would have been something of a rarity, today he or she is seen as the norm. The mountain bike has re-focused peoples' attention on cycling and it is no longer the BMX or sports bike (or any other items of leisure equipment for that matter) that are on the top of the Christmas present list for kids – first and foremost lies the mountain bike.

As youngsters are the purchasers of tomorrow the continued growth of mountain biking is all but guaranteed. Mountain bikes also appeal to other age groups whose attention span is longer. A convert who is older than eighteen is likely to be an enthusiast for the rest of his or her life. This is where mountain biking is different to such fads as BMX, pogo sticks and skateboards – the sport is undertaken by adults who have the potential to enjoy it for as long as they remain healthy and active.

The advent, and demise, of under-the-bar shifters has shown that gearing will continue to evolve and likewise further advances in frame materials are likely but the steps forward will be hops rather than leaps.

Basically the future lies in refinements not in radical departures. Certainly such composite materials as aluminium mixed with carbon or boron fibre will become more popular with manufacturers looking for eye-catching sales gimmicks, but the steel alloy frames will continue to be the standard. The bike of today is unlikely to change all that much. It is only on the custom side that huge differences will be noticeable. The standard Taiwanese mountain bike is modelled on a Tom Ritchey machine which was inspired by Californian conditions. Yet it is only the custom builders who have recognised that this Californian design is not perfect for other locations. Even within America there were always differences in frame configurations and so forth. One such design – the 'Seattle' type – was inspired by the riding conditions of northwest America, where it was best for bottom brackets to be high in order that the bike could clear the many arboreal obstacles that lay across the miles and miles of indigenous logging tracks. Similarly British custom builders have long recognised that conditions over here are a touch different from California, and such people as Geoff Apps and David Wrath-Sharman have designed bikes that are very British in provenance and style. This sector of the bike market may expand. Larger manufacturers may increase their output of gentler, less extreme bikes that can cope with British conditions slightly better than the steep-angled Californian bikes. This sector of the market will still be tiny but certainly the custom building of bikes will

The mountain bike is the bike carrying cycling into the future.

Further advances in frame materials are likely.

The standard Taiwanese mountain bike.

increase. Experienced riders soon spot the shortcomings of the standardised product and recognise that custom builders can construct bikes more suited to their own riding style.

The major manufacturers will concentrate on consolidating their hold on the lower levels of the market. They will attempt to further standardise the mountain bike – for reasons of economy of scale. However, to continue to capture the attention of serious riders, the major manufacturers will still have to pay lip-service to the new gimmicks and advances that the Japanese are so happy to churn out. At the lower end of the market, bike designs and set-ups will remain fairly static. The medium-sized manufacturers will take up the radical new suggestions of the custom builders and bikes may get more and more sophisticated. The aspirational young people who buy mountain bikes will still have huge appetites for new fangled machinery. Constant changes in design and componentary will mean a steady rate of sales at the upper end of the market.

Mountain bike couriers will increase in popularity.

The real growth however, will come from the large manufacturers who will continue to sell the concept of radical mountain bikes to Mr and Mrs Average, but instead of giving them a radical mountain bike, that they would have little use for, they will carry on giving them pseudo-machines.

Bicycle ownership will increase enormously. The Green movement will mean that more bikes will be used than ever before. The dreams of such bodies as Transport 2000 and the Friends of the Earth – for more bikes and less cars – will go some way towards fruition. The next ten years will see the mountain bike go from strength to strength. The amount of die-hard off-roaders will increase steadily but not dramatically. The majority of riders will be, in effect, 'street mountain bikers' and it is here that the most potential lies; sales to this segment will continue to sky-rocket. Gradually more and more of these street mountain bikers will attempt to live up to their off-road image and the countryside may fill to overflowing with riders and their machines. As long as we tread carefully over the domain of walkers, horse riders and other countryside users then the hills and dales should remain open to us.

For the sake of the future of mountain biking we need to inculcate responsible attitudes towards the outdoors. If we do not and access starts to become not just a problem but a nightmare, then the mountain bike may become little more than an anarchronism, a misfit with nowhere to go but the tarmac. However, I doubt that this will happen. Mountain biking is too strong a sport for outside pressures to squeeze it into new and unwelcome directions. Too many peoples' imaginations have been captured. The adventure and fun element is just too powerful.

Mountain biking will survive into the next century as vibrant – if not even more so – than any one of the new adventure sports that have appeared over the last few years. Also, given its very wide user base, it will possibly become as strong as many of the more traditional pastimes such as recreational walking and going to the match on a Saturday. It will certainly attract more television coverage and this in turn will bring new people into the sport. A steady throughflow of new blood will help to keep mountain biking a lively, fresh and attractive activity.

# VIEWPOINTS

*Where do you see mountain biking in five to ten years time?*

**Drew Lawson** 'There are two possible courses – either it will continue to grow at this ridiculous rate or it will peak at some stage and dip a bit. It is not going to disappear though – it

149

The adventure and fun element is just too powerful.

Mountain biking is a fresh and attractive outdoor activity.

Hopefully the sun will never set on mountain biking.

will still be a healthy fifty per cent at least, of the market even when it does dip because mountain biking is a functional, fun thing – it is not just a fashionable thing it is a purpose filling sport. Like windsurfing it is a function in itself – it is something you do. Windsurfing is not a weird offshoot of surfing it is a sport in itself. And mountain biking is similarly a sport in itself.'

*Is componentary likely to get better and better in the future?*

**Drew Lawson** 'Most of the leaps and bounds in componentary so far have been by Shimano and their dominance of the market is dictated by being ahead – they cannot afford not to come up with new ideas or improvements. Once they have invented something, within a year or two it has been copied – so they have to progress to keep their market share. Frame designs, on the other hand, are as close as possible now to being perfect.

Everybody who is in the game – whether they make tyres or spokes or rims or frames or saddles – if they want to do well they must come up with better goods. And it is a growing market, a more competitive market, so everything is going to continue to improve. When the market flattens out there will be too many people in the game and the prices will drop and then progress will slow down.'

151

# Further Reading

Clayden, P. and Trevelyan, J., *Rights of Way: a Guide to Law and Practice* (Open Spaces Society and the Rambler's Association, 1983).

Cliff, P., *Mountain Navigation* (Cordee, 1986).

Constance, H., *Gear for the Outdoors and How to Make it* (Robert Hale, 1982).

Crane, R. and Crane, N., *Bicycles Up Kilimanjaro* (OUP, 1985).

Garner, J. F., *Garner's Rights of Way* (Longman, 1989).

Garner, J. F. and Jones, B. L., *Countryside Law* (Shaw & Sons, 1987).

Glaskin, M. and Torr, J., *Mountain Biking* (Pelham Books, 1988).

Harley, J. B., *Ordnance Survey Maps: a Descriptive Manual* (Ordnance Survey, 1975).

Horton, N., *Cycling Off-road and the Law* (Bicycle Action and the Cyclists Touring Club, 1987).

Kelly, C. and Crane, N., *Richard's Mountain Bike Book* (OUP, 1988).

Langmuir, E., *Mountaincraft and Leadership: a Handbook for Mountaineers and Hillwalking Leaders* (Scottish Sports Council and Mountain Leadership Training Board, 1984).

Lynn, I. and others, *The Off-Road Bicycle Book* (Leading Edge, 1987).

McInnes, H., *International Mountain Rescue Handbook* (Constable, 1972).

Neve, R., *Simply Map Reading* (Ordnance Survey and Telegraph Maps, 1988).

Pedgley, D. E., *Mountain Weather: a Practical Guide for Hillwalkers and Climbers in the British Isles* (Cicerone Press, 1979).

Renouf, J. and Hulse, S., *First Aid for Hill Walkers & Climbers* (Cicerone Press, 1982).

Ricketts, B., *The Mountain Biking Handbook* (Arena Press, 1988).

*Rights of Way: a Guide to the Law of Scotland* (Scottish Rights of Way Society Ltd, 1986).

Sloane, E., *Eugene Sloane's Complete Book of All-terrain Bicycles* (Simon & Schuster, 1985).

Van der Plas, R., *The Mountain Bike Book* (Velo Press, 1984).

Walker, K., *Mountain Navigation Techniques* (Constable, 1986).

Whittet, A. and Stewart, P., *The Bridleways of Britain* (Whittet Books, 1987).

Wilson, J. G., *Follow the Map: the Ordnance Survey Guide* (A & C Black and the Ordnance Survey, 1987).

# Useful Addresses

## ORGANISATIONS

**Association for the Protection of Rural Scotland,** 14a Napier Road, Edinburgh, EH10 5AY.

**British Trust for Conservation Volunteers,** 36 St Mary's Street, Wallingford, Oxfordshire, OX10 0EU.

**British Waterways Board,** Melbury House, Melbury Terrace, London, NW1.

**By-ways and Bridleway Trust,** 9 Queen Anne's Gate, London, SW1H 9BY.

**Council for the Protection of Rural England,** 4 Hobart Place, London, SW1W 0PT.

**Council for the Protection of Rural Wales (Cymdethas Diogelu Cyru Wiedig),** 31 High Street, Welshpool, Powys, SY21 7JP.

**Countryside Commission,** John Dower House, Crescent Place, Cheltenham, Gloucestershire, GL50 3RA.

**Cross-country Cycling Club,** 5 Old Station Cottages, Ford, Arundel, West Sussex, BN18 0BJ.

**Expedition Advisory Service,** Tel: 01 581 2057

**Forestry Commission,** 231 Corstorphine Road, Edinburgh, EH12 7AT.

**Friends of the Earth,** 26–28 Underwood Street, London, N1 7JQ.

**Hospital for Tropical Diseases,** 3 St Pancras Way, London NW1.

**Mountain Bike Club,** Santon House, Santon Downham, Suffolk.

**Mountain Bothies Association,** 2 North Gardner Street, Glasgow, G11 5BT.

**Open Spaces Society,** 25a Bell Street, Henley-on-Thames, Oxfordshire, RG9 2BA.

**Ordnance Survey,** Romsey Road, Maybush, Southampton, Hampshire, SO9 4DH.

**Rough Stuff Fellowship,** 55 Grafton Road, New Malden, Surrey, KT3 3AA.

**Scottish Rights of Way Society,** 1 Lutton Place, Edinburgh, EH8 9PD.

**Scottish Sports Council,** 1 St Colme Street, Edinburgh, EH3 6AA.

**Scottish Youth Hostels Association,** 7 Glebe Crescent, Stirling, FK8 2JA.

**Stanford Map Shop,** 12–14 Long Acre, Covent Garden, London, WC2E 9LP.

**Sports Council,** 16 Upper Woburn Place, London, WC1H 0QP.

**Sports Council (Northern Ireland),** House of Sport, Upper Malone Road, Belfast, BT9 5LA.

**Trail Riders Fellowship,** 29 Anderson Drive, Kettering, Northamptonshire, NN15 5DG.

**Transport 2000,** Walkden House, Melton Street, London, NW1.

**Visa Shop,** 44 Chandos Place, London, WC2.

**Visaservice,** 2 Northdown Street, Kings Cross, London, N1.

**Youth Hostels Association,** Trevalyan House, 8 St Stephen's Hill, St Albans, Hertfordshire, AL1 2DY.

**Youth Hostels Association of Northern Ireland,** 56 Bradbury Place, Belfast, BT7 1RU.

# MOUNTAIN BIKE COMPANIES – BIKES AND ACCESSORIES

**British Eagle,** P. O. Box 6, Eagle Cycle Works, Mochdre, Newtown, Powys, SY16 4LD.

**Campagnolo S. p. A.** (*Groupsets*), Via delle Chimica 4, 36100 Vicenza, Italy.

**Caratti Sport Ltd** (*Specialized, Vetta, Tioga*), Unit 49, Waverley Road, Beeches Industrial Estate, Yate, Bristol, Avon, BS17 5QZ.

**CAT MTBs,** Astonocean, Unit 6d, Pomon Road, Long Rock Industrial Estate, Penzance, Cornwall.

**Chainsport Distributors Ltd** (*Fisher, Cannondale*), 40–2 Clapham High Street, Clapham, London, SW4 7UR.

**Cleland Cycles Ltd,** 5 Old Station Cottages, Ford, Arundel, West Sussex, BN18 0BJ.

**Cycles Peugeot Ltd,** Edison Road, Bedford, Bedfordshire, MK41 0HU.

**Cycle Rims & Accessories** (*Stronglight*), 18 The Ridgeway, Wimbledon, London, SW19 4QN.

**Dawes Cycles Ltd,** Wharf Road, Tyseley, Birmingham, West Midlands, B11 2EA.

**Diamond Back & Emmelle,** Moore Large & Company, Daleside Road Industrial Estate, Poulton Drive, Nottingham, Nottinghamshire, NG2 4BN.

**Falcon Cycles Ltd,** P. O. Box 3, Bridge Street, Brigg, Humberside, DN20 8PB.

**Fisher Mountain Bikes,** 140 Mitchel Building, San Rafael, CA 94903, USA.

**Giant UK Ltd,** Plessey Business Park, Technology Drive, Beeston, Nottingham, Nottinghamshire, NG9 2ND.

**Highpath,** 54 Highpath Road, Merrow, Guildford, Surrey, GU1 2QQ.

**Horizon,** Two Wheels Good, 35 Call Lane, Leeds, West Yorkshire, LS1 7BT.

**Kitching, Ron** (*SunTour* and other items from a mail order catalogue), Hookstone Park, Harrogate, North Yorkshire, HG2 7BZ.

**Kona, Second Level Sport Ltd,** Clockhouse Lane, Bedfont, Feltham, Middlesex, TW14 8QA.

**Madison Cycles Plc** (*Ridgeback, Shimano* and other items from a mail order catalogue), 4 Horseshoe Close, London, NW2 7JJ.

**Marin,** ATB Sales, Highfield Drive, Churchfield Industrial Estate, St Leonards, Sussex.

**MBK Bicycles,** Moore Large & Company, Crown House, 664–668 Dunstable Road, Luton, Bedfordshire, LU4 8SD.

**Mongoose,** Hot Wheels International, 1145 Christchurch Road, Bournemouth, Dorset, BH7 3BW.

**MS Racing,** MCCF, Unit 11, East Park Trading Estate, Gordon Road, Whitehall, Bristol, Avon, BS5 7DH.

**Muddy Fox & Kiss Miami,** 331 Athlon Road, Wembley, Middlesex, HA0 1BY.

**Orange Mountain Bikes,** 148 Hanson Lane, Halifax, West Yorkshire.

**Outsider,** The Bicycle Chain, 10 Bradbury Street, London, N16 8JN.

**Overbury's,** 138 Ashley Road, Bristol, Avon.

**Pace Research,** 62 Toller Lane, Bradford, West Yorkshire, BD8 9BY.

**Raleigh Ltd,** Triumph Road, Nottingham, Nottinghamshire, NG7 2DD.

**Reflex Mountain Bike Company,** Unit C, The Gate Studios, Station Road, Elstree, Borehamwood, London.

**Roberts,** Chas Roberts Cycles, 89 Gloucester Road, Croydon, Surrey, CR0 2DN.

**Saracen Cycles Ltd,** Saracen House, Harriott Drive, Heathcote Industrial Estate, Warwick, CV34 6TS.

**Scott USA,** Bert Harkins Racing, Unit 6, The Townsend Centre, Houghton Regis, Nr Dunstable, Bedfordshire.

**Serval Marketing Ltd** (*Oakley* sunglasses), Serval House, Clifton Road, Sheffield, Bedfordshire, SG17 5BZ.

**Stronglight,** BP222, 54 Boulevard Fauriat, 42005, St Etienne Cedex, France.

**Sturmy Archer Ltd,** Triumph Road, Nottingham, Nottinghamshire, NG7 2GL.

**Swallow Cycles,** 2 Stannetts, Laindon North Trade Centre, Essex, SS15 6DJ.

**Swinnerton, Roy,** 67–71 Victoria Road, Fenton, Stoke-on-Trent, Staffordshire.

**Tip-Top Vulcanising Products Ltd,** Westland Square, Leeds, West Yorkshire, LS11 5XS.

**Off-Road** (bikes and *Flexstem*), Ultrasport Ltd, Acton Grove, Acton Road Industrial Estate, Long Eaton, Nottingham, Nottinghamshire, NG10 1FY.

**Yates, Dave,** c/o M. Steel Cycles, 2 Station Road, South Gosforth, Newcastle upon Tyne, Tyne and Wear.

# CLOTHING

**Been Bag Cycle Clothing Ltd,** Unit 8D, No. 1 Industrial Estate, Medomsley Road, Consett, County Durham.

**Berghaus,** 34 Dean Street, Newcastle upon Tyne, Tyne and Wear, NE1 1PG.

**Calange Outdoor Clothing,** Harditex House, Davenport Avenue, Withington, Manchester, M20 9EZ.

**Fast,** MCCF, Unit 11, East Park Trading Estate, Gordon Road, Whitehall, Bristol, Avon, BS5 7DH.

**Field and Trek,** 23/25 Kings Road, Brentwood, Essex.

**Helly Hansen (UK) Ltd,** College Street, Kempston, Bedford, Bedfordshire, MK42 8NA.

**Ron Hill Sports,** P. O. Box 11, Hyde, Cheshire.

**Karrimor International,** Petre Road, Clayton le Moors, Accrington, Lancashire, BB5 5JP.

**Mountain Equipment,** Leech Street, Stalybridge, Cheshire, SK15 1SD.

**Polaris Clothing,** 218 Meadowhead, Sheffield, South Yorkshire, S8 0PG.

**Rohan,** 30 Maryland Road, Tongwell, Milton Keynes, Bedfordshire, MK15 8HN.

**Snow and Rock,** 188 Kensington High Street, London W8.

**Sprayway,** 16 Chester Street, Manchester, M1 5GE.

**Survival Aids,** Morland, Penrith, Cumbria, CA10 3AZ.

**Swallow,** 2 Stannetts, Laindon North Trade Centre, Essex, SS15 6DJ.

# Index

Italic numerals denote page numbers of illustrations

# OTHER CYCLING BOOKS FROM THE CROWOOD PRESS

## Cycle Sport

**Peter Konopka**

Fully illustrated throughout in both colour and black and white, and with clear detailed line-drawings, Peter Konopka discusses every possible aspect of the sport including the history of cycling, equipment, training, recovery, diet, competition and health.

160 pages        ISBN 1 85223 280 3

## Touring Bikes

**Tony Oliver**

The ideal guide to the technical world of cycle touring. Tony Oliver uses his enthusiasm and experience to show you how to choose the perfect touring machine. Highly illustrated with both line-drawings and black and white photographs, *Touring Bikes* is designed for both the aspiring and regular tourist.

160 pages        ISBN 1 85223 339 7

## Offroad Adventure Cycling

**Jeremy Evans**

50 routes in England, suitable for the owners of all-terrain bikes, described in detail with maps, places for refreshment and points of interest. Ideal day trips for the adventurous cyclist.

192 pages        ISBN 1 85223 368 0